ROY BENNETT

Discovering Music

BOOK ONE

LONGMAN

The orchestra

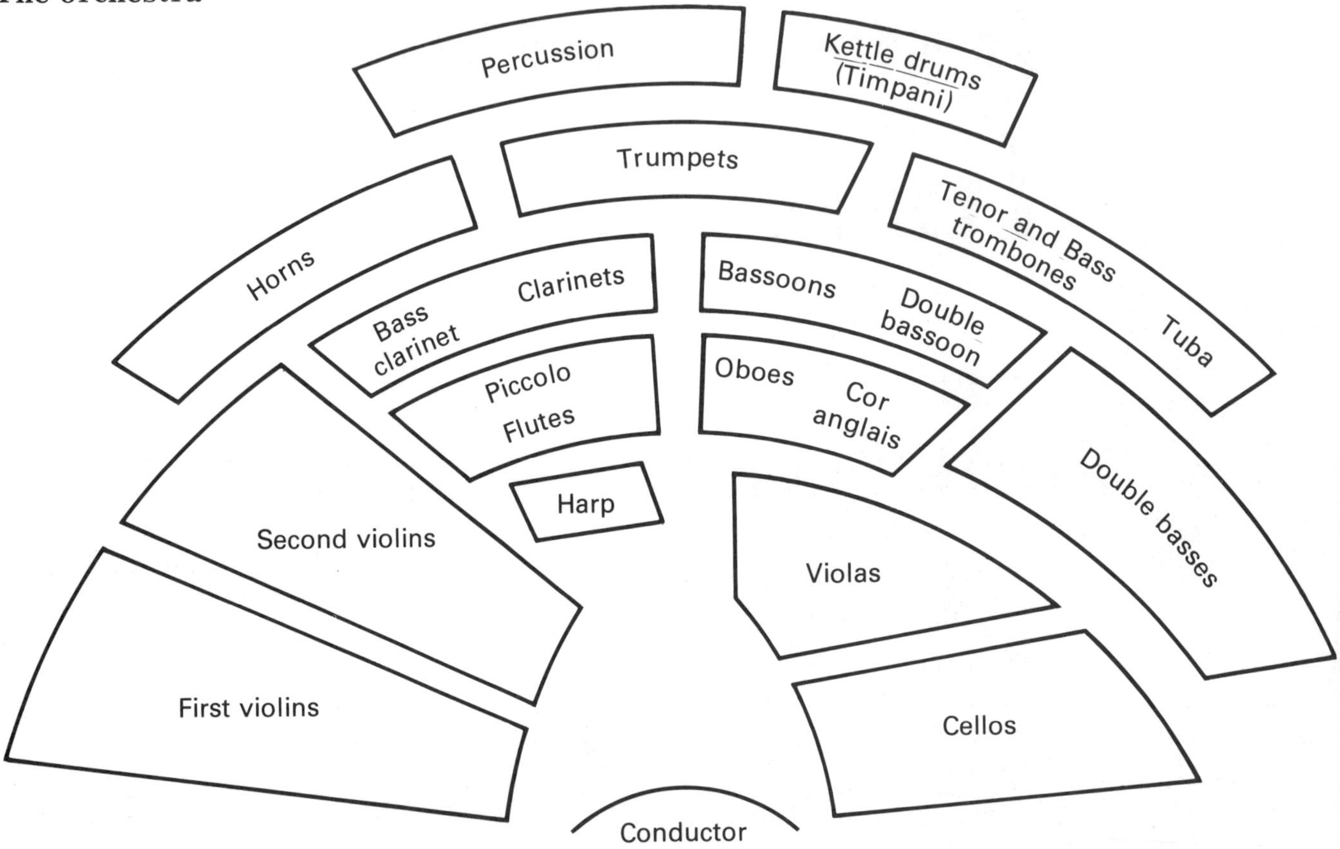

Percussion

Kettle drums
(Timpani)

Trumpets

Horns

Tenor and Bass
trombones

Bass
clarinet

Clarinets

Bassoons

Double
bassoon

Tuba

Piccolo
Flutes

Oboes

Cor
anglais

Harp

Double basses

Second violins

Violas

First violins

Cellos

Conductor

HENRY PURCELL

1659–1695 ENGLAND

Henry Purcell (signature)

Henry Purcell is considered to be one of the greatest English composers. He came from a very musical family. His father and his uncle were both singers of the Chapel Royal. His brother Daniel also became a composer, and was very famous for his organ playing. And both his son and his grandson later became composers.

Purcell was born in London. We are not sure of the exact date, but it was probably during the year 1659. So as a boy, he lived through both the Great Plague (1665) and the Great Fire of · London (1666).

At the age of eight or so, he was a singer of the Chapel Royal. When his voice broke, he left to become 'assistant keeper, maker, repairer, mender and tuner of the King's Instruments' – the King being Charles II. In 1677, he was appointed 'Composer in Ordinary to the Royal Household'. Two years later, he became organist at Westminster Abbey and, in 1682, of the Chapel Royal as well.

The music Purcell composed during his short but busy life is extremely varied. His official duties meant he had to provide music for many royal occasions – pieces for royal birthdays and funerals, and 'Welcome Songs' to celebrate the return to London after a royal journey. And as organist, he was expected to compose music for the church, such as anthems. But besides all this, he found time to write many songs and instrumental pieces and, in particular, a great deal of music for the theatre.

The beginning of a Sonata by Purcell

When he died, in 1695, Purcell was buried 'in a magnificent manner' in Westminster Abbey, close to the organ he had played during the last sixteen years of his life.

Hornpipe, from the Seventh Suite for harpsichord

Purcell's eight *Suites* (or 'groups of pieces') for harpsichord are mostly made up of dances. Originally, a 'hornpipe' was a single-reed woodwind instrument found in certain parts of the British Isles. It was used to provide music for a lively dance, chiefly associated with sailors. But later on, the name 'hornpipe' came to describe the dance itself.

Purcell's *Hornpipe* is built up in *binary* (or 'two-part') form. The music is in two sections, and each of these is repeated:

$$\|\!\!: \ \mathbf{A} \ :\|\!\!: \ \mathbf{B} \ :\|$$

The harpsichord

The strings of the harpsichord are plucked. When a key is pressed down, a strip of wood called a *jack* jumps up inside the harpsichord, and a *plectrum* plucks the string. Many harpsichords have two keyboards and two, or even more, complete sets of strings and jacks.

It is not possible to make the sounds on a harpsichord grow *gradually* louder or softer (as you can on a piano). But it is possible to vary them. Plectrums made of quill produce a bright, rich sound. Leather plectrums are softer and warmer sounding. Pulling out one of the 'stops' may allow two sets of strings to be played from one keyboard, making a louder, fuller sound. A 'lute stop' causes jacks to pluck nearer to the ends of strings, giving a softer, thinner tone.

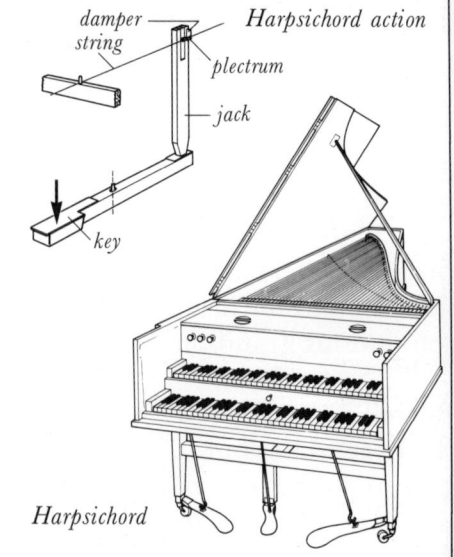

Harpsichord

Trumpet Overture, from 'The Indian Queen'

The Indian Queen was a play for which Purcell composed songs and orchestral pieces. The story of the play takes place in Mexico in the 16th century, and tells how Queen Zempoalla plots to snatch the throne from Montezuma, last Emperor of the Aztecs.

This *Trumpet Overture* introduces Act 3 of the play (*overture* means 'opening piece'). The music is in three contrasting sections:

1. A slow, very majestic introduction in a strong, rather jerky rhythm (Tune **A**, below).

2. The main, faster section of the Overture. Instruments enter in turn, playing Tune **B**:
   first violins – closely followed by
   second violins;
   violas;
   cellos and basses, with harpsichord;
   violins again;
   and finally, trumpet.
   Later on, listen for the first four notes of Tune **B** (marked in the bracket) to be tossed to and fro between trumpet and strings.

3. The Overture ends with slow, quiet music in which the trumpet is silent.

The trumpet

In Purcell's day, the trumpet had no valves and (like a bugle) could only play certain notes. A player had to find these notes by changing the pressure of his lips against the mouthpiece. The higher the note – the tighter his lips had to be.

It was not until early in the 19th century, when valves were invented, that other notes became possible. Now, on the modern trumpet, each of the three valves brings in an extra length of tubing – offering other whole series of notes. By using valves in different combinations, and also varying his lip pressure, a modern trumpet player can play any note throughout the range of his instrument.

Sometimes, for a different kind of sound, a trumpeter fits a *mute* into the bell of his trumpet.

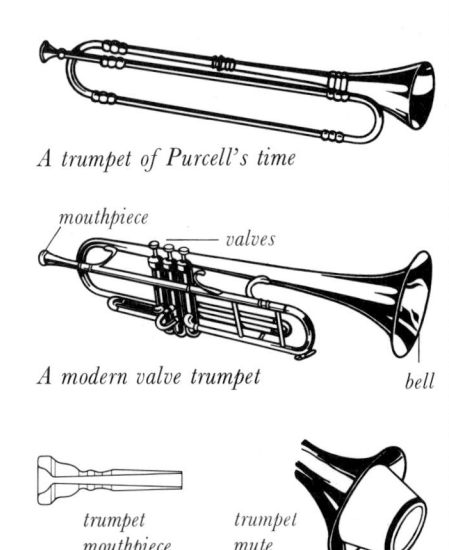

A trumpet of Purcell's time

A modern valve trumpet

trumpet mouthpiece   *trumpet mute*

Handel was born in 1685 (the same year as another great German composer, Bach), in Halle. His father intended that he should become a lawyer, but Handel became a violinist and harpsichord player at the opera house in Hamburg and, by the time he was twenty, had seen his first opera performed there.

He travelled to Italy – the leading musical country at that time – and stayed for five years, learning a great deal from the music he heard there. His own compositions, especially operas and church music, earned him high praise and when he returned home, he was recognised as a composer of brilliant talent.

In 1710, Handel visited England where he found Italian opera was all the rage. In just two weeks, he composed an opera called *Rinaldo*, which was performed with immediate success.

Returning to Germany, Handel took the post of *Kapellmeister* – or 'director of music' – at the court of the Elector of Hanover. After a year, he asked permission to visit England again, promising to return 'within a reasonable time'. But success and fame in London made life in Hanover seem very dull and unexciting. Handel decided to stay on – and in fact, remained in England for the rest of his life.

Then, in 1714, Queen Anne died. Her successor to the throne of England was none other than Handel's rightful employer, the Elector of Hanover, who now became King George I. This was rather embarrassing for Handel. He was now accepted as England's leading composer and so a meeting with the King could hardly be avoided.

At first, the King was angry at Handel's long absence from his court in Hanover. But he eventually forgave him. For a long time, it was believed that this came about on an occasion when the King and his court made a journey up the river Thames on the royal barge. Handel followed in another boat, filled with musicians playing pieces he had written which he called the *Water Music*.

The King, surprised and delighted by the music he heard echoing across the water, was said to have had Handel brought to him, and to have forgiven him there and then. But this is no longer held to be true. Handel did indeed compose the *Water Music* for a royal water-party on the Thames – but by then he had already regained favour with the King.

Suite: The Water Music

Handel's *Water Music* consists of twenty pieces altogether. You will often hear just a handful of these performed as a *suite* (or group of pieces) arranged by the conductor, Sir Hamilton Harty.

Allegro ('rather quickly')
In this piece, Handel contrasts different 'blocks' of sound, one against another. First we hear horns alternating with the rest of the orchestra; then woodwind alternating with strings:

You can imagine the splendid effect of this music by Handel – especially the horn calls – echoing distantly across the water from his boat of musicians.

A musical water-party on the Thames, painted by Zoffany

The early horn

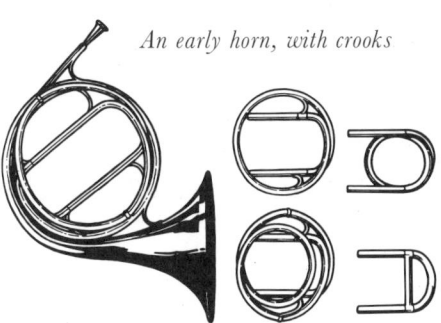

An early horn, with crooks

Until valves were invented, the horn (like the early trumpet) could play only those notes available from a single length of brass tubing. A player could alter the total length by changing *crooks*. These were extra bits of tubing, graded in size. But although a different crook provided a new *range* of notes, the actual *number* available was exactly the same.

Here are three more pieces from Handel's *Water Music*:

Bourrée
A fast, crisp dance-tune with two main beats in each bar:

Hornpipe
Another lively dance, this time with three fast beats to a bar:

Allegro deciso ('rather quickly, and decisively')
Handel builds up this piece in what is called *ternary* form. *Ternary* means 'three', and so the music is arranged in three sections. The first and third sections are made from the same music (**A**). The second section (Music **B**) presents a contrast of some kind in the middle – making a kind of 'musical sandwich':

Music **A**	Music **B** (a contrast)	Music **A** again

Here are the two tunes, **A** and **B**, used by Handel in this piece:

Music **A** soon brings in the exciting sounds of horns, trumpets and drums. Music **B** presents a contrast, and is for strings and woodwind only. Then Music **A** returns to end the piece.

Hallelujah Chorus, from 'Messiah'

Handel's *Messiah* is an *oratorio*. In an oratorio, the composer sets religious words (usually from the Bible) for choir and solo singers, accompanied by an orchestra. Unlike an opera, there are no costumes or scenery. An oratorio is not acted – it is just sung.

Of the many oratorios which Handel composed, *Messiah* is the most famous. It is a very long work, taking a whole evening to perform – yet Handel completed it in the amazingly short time of only twenty-four days. King George II was present at the first London performance of *Messiah* which took place in 1743.

The best-known piece from *Messiah* is the *Hallelujah Chorus*. (*Hallelujah* is a Hebrew word meaning 'Praise be to God'.)

The music begins with a short introduction for the orchestra; and then the choir bursts in, singing joyful 'Hallelujahs' (Music **A**).

Then follow the words: 'For the Lord God Omnipotent reigneth' (Music **B**). At this moment, the King was so impressed by Handel's music that he rose to his feet. This, of course, caused the entire audience to stand as well – so setting a tradition which is still followed to this day.

The final page of Handel's 'Messiah'; the crossings-out show how quickly he worked

The house in Lower Brook Street where Handel composed 'Messiah'

Arrival of the Queen of Sheba, from 'Solomon'

Solomon was one of the last oratorios which Handel composed, and this lively orchestral piece has been given this title since it begins Part 3 of the oratorio, when the Queen of Sheba arrives bringing gifts of gold, spices and precious stones to King Solomon.

Bustling strings announce the approach of the royal procession:

On several occasions during the music, Handel gives the two oboes fanfare-like solos to play:

The oboe

This woodwind instrument has a double reed – two pieces of cane, shaved at one end to a wafer thinness. When the player blows between them, the two reeds vibrate against each other, giving the oboe its characteristic, 'reedy' tone.

The oboe can sound sad in slow, smooth melodies; but perky and biting if given a fast, rhythmic tune to play.

The cor anglais, or English horn, is really a large kind of oboe with a deeper voice.

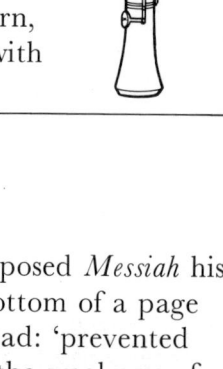

Handel conducting an oratorio

Not long after Handel had composed *Messiah* his eyesight began to fail. At the bottom of a page of one of his compositions we read: 'prevented from proceeding on account of the weakness of my left eye'.

In spite of several operations, Handel became totally blind. He continued to compose, however, relying on his secretary and music copyist, Christopher Smith, to write down the notes for him.

Handel died on April 14th, 1759. He was buried in Westminster Abbey, and it was said that three thousand people attended his funeral service.

George Frideric Handel

JOSEPH HAYDN

1732–1809   AUSTRIA

Haydn was born the son of a wheelwright in the small village of Rohrau in Lower Austria. He was one of twelve children. The family was poor but musical, and in the evenings the children would often enjoy singing while their father accompanied them on the harp.

At eight years old, Haydn became a choirboy at St. Stephen's Cathedral in Vienna. When his voice broke, at seventeen, he was forced to leave the choir, and decided to rent a tiny attic in Vienna. For a time, he managed to earn his living by composing, playing and teaching.

When he was twenty-nine, Haydn was offered the post of *Kapellmeister* – or 'director of music' – to a rich Hungarian family named Esterházy. He now found himself in charge of an orchestra, choir, and many capable solo musicians. Each week, he was expected to compose, rehearse and conduct a vast amount of music – including orchestral and instrumental pieces for the palace concert room, operas for the Esterházy private theatre, and religious music for services in the

Josephus Haydn

The Esterházy Castle in Hungary

chapel. With so many capable musicians at hand, Haydn was able to try out new musical ideas and immediately judge their effect, altering and adjusting his music as he thought fit.

Haydn remained with the Esterházy family for thirty years. Then, when Prince Nicholas Esterházy died, he returned to Vienna. He continued to compose. He twice visited England, each time taking with him six symphonies for performance at concerts in London arranged by an impresario named Salomon. These, the last twelve of Haydn's 104 symphonies, are called the '*London*', or '*Salomon*', *Symphonies*. Haydn himself conducted them from the keyboard, as was the fashion at that time.

Haydn conducting from the keyboard

Second Movement from Symphony No. 100 in G (the 'Military' Symphony)

Haydn was one of the earliest composers to write symphonies. A symphony is a fairly lengthy work for full orchestra. It is usually made up of four separate pieces called 'movements', each one different in speed and mood.

This is how a composer of Haydn's time might plan out a symphony:

1st movement: fairly fast (but perhaps beginning with a slow introduction)
2nd movement: slower, and often song-like
3rd movement: a minuet and trio (the minuet was a popular 18th-century dance with three beats to a bar)
4th movement (*Finale*): at a fast pace

In Haydn's day, the only percussion instruments heard in symphonies were kettle drums (often called *timpani*). His *Symphony No. 100* was given the nickname 'Military' because it brings in extra percussion during the second and fourth movements. So as well as kettle drums, we hear triangle, cymbals and bass drum – instruments at that time associated with a military band rather than a symphony orchestra.

Besides percussion, the orchestra needed to perform Haydn's *'Military' Symphony* includes:

Strings	Woodwind	Brass
first violins	1 flute	2 horns
second violins	2 oboes	2 trumpets
violas	2 clarinets	
cellos	2 bassoons	
double basses		

Kettle drums (or timpani) are copper bowls with skin stretched tightly across the top. Tightening or slackening the skin raises or lowers the pitch of the note. The player can make single strokes, or he can play a 'roll' by using both sticks alternately and very quickly. Haydn used a pair of kettle drums in his orchestra. Nowadays there are three, or even more.

The **triangle** is a steel rod bent into the shape of a triangle but with one corner left open. The player can make separate 'tings', or play a *trill* by rattling the metal beater inside the top corner.

The big, **bass drum** gives out a low, booming noise rather than a clearly pitched note like the kettle drum. You may hear single 'booms', or a thunderous roll played with kettle drum sticks.

Cymbals are metal dishes which may be clashed against each other, or brushed gently together. A single suspended cymbal may be struck or rolled with drum sticks, hard or soft.

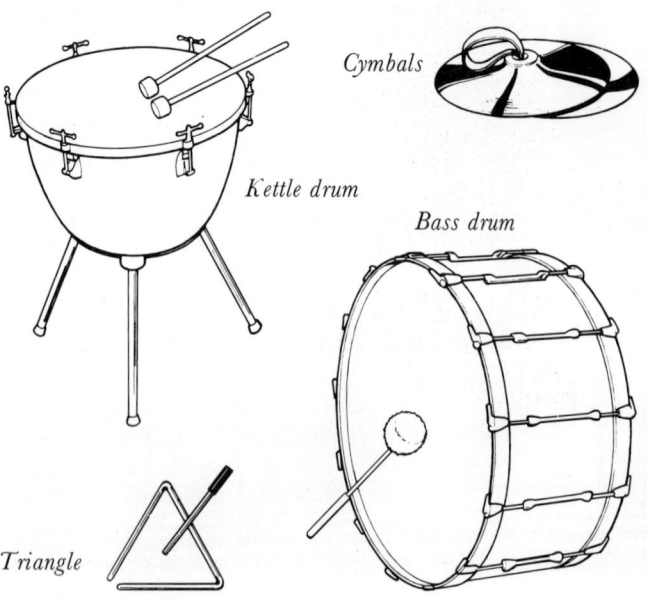

Cymbals

Kettle drum

Bass drum

Triangle

The second movement from Haydn's '*Military*' *Symphony* is built up in four sections. All four are based on this tune:

1. The first section is mainly for strings and woodwind. The tune is played first by violins and flute.
2. A sudden contrast! This second section uses the full orchestra, including the extra percussion instruments, and begins with the opening snatch of the tune (marked in the bracket), but played now in the *minor* key.
3. This section is very similar to the first – but makes more use of the full orchestra.
4. The movement ends with a *coda* (Italian for 'tail', or 'rounding-off'). It begins with a fanfare for the two trumpets.

'*Gypsy*' *Rondo, from Piano Trio No. 25 in G major*

This lively music was given this nickname because it has much of the flavour and high spirits found in Hungarian gypsy dances. *Trio* means 'three', and the three instruments you will hear in a piano trio are a piano, a violin, and a cello.

Haydn designs this piece in *rondo* form. In a rondo, the main tune keeps coming round, with other, contrasting, tunes heard in between. This is the main tune of Haydn's '*Gypsy*' *Rondo*:

Joseph Haydn

Get to know this main tune first. Then listen for it as you hear a complete performance of this Rondo. How many times does the main tune come round?

Variations, from the 'Emperor' String Quartet

A *quartet* is music for four players, and the four instruments which play a string quartet are 2 violins, 1 viola and 1 cello. Like a symphony, a string quartet is usually made up of four separate movements.

Haydn composed more than 80 string quartets, of which the 'Emperor' is No. 77. It earned this nickname because, in the second movement, Haydn writes variations on a hymn tune he had once composed for the birthday of the Austrian Emperor. You may already know this tune. It was once the Austrian national anthem, but is now the national anthem of West Germany. And it is still often sung as a hymn tune to the words 'Glorious things of Thee are spoken'.

In this movement from Haydn's *'Emperor' String Quartet* we first hear this tune played by the first violin, while the second violin, viola and cello provide a hymn-like accompaniment.

Then Haydn writes four *variations* in which each instrument in the quartet plays the tune in turn. Haydn makes no alterations to the tune itself, but he disguises it each time by varying – or changing – the accompaniment in some new and interesting way.

This is what happens in each of the four variations:

Variation 1. The tune is now heard on the second violin against a running accompaniment in quicker notes, played by the first violin alone.

Variation 2. The cello takes over the tune. The second violin and the viola quietly accompany while the first violin weaves a descant, high above.

Variation 3. The tune passes to the viola. It is accompanied at first by the two violins, but later the cello joins in as well.

Variation 4. In this last variation, Haydn alters the harmonies, making the music sound more wistful. The tune is given to the first violin, soon soaring high above the other three instruments.

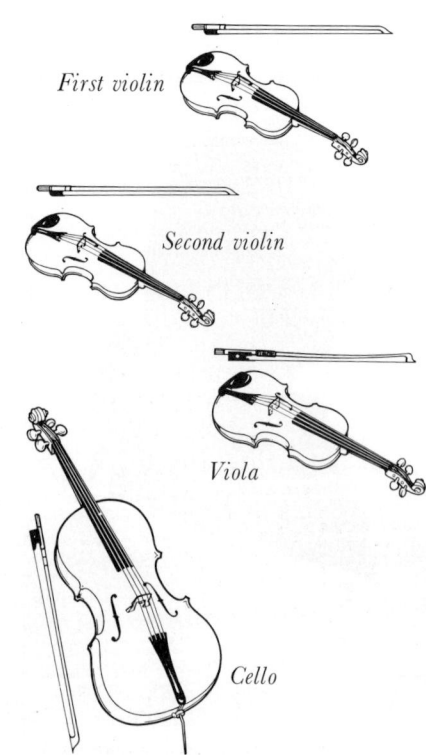

First violin

Second violin

Viola

Cello

LUDWIG VAN BEETHOVEN

1770–1827 GERMANY

Beethoven's childhood was miserably unhappy. His father, who was a singer by profession, was determined that his son should swiftly become famous as a child musician. And so Beethoven was taught to play the piano and the violin from the age of four. He was severely beaten if he didn't practise enough. Sometimes his father would arrive home late from the tavern, very drunk. He would drag the boy from his bed and force him to practise at the piano.

Beethoven had his first composition published when he was eleven. At seventeen, he went to Vienna where he played to Mozart, who said: 'Watch this young man – he will make a great noise in the world!'. Later, for a short time, Beethoven took composition lessons from Haydn in Vienna.

Beethoven soon became famous in Vienna, both as pianist and composer. His music made a strong impact upon audiences. Listeners accustomed to the polished, 'polite' music of Haydn and Mozart found Beethoven's music often took them unawares. It appealed strongly to the emotions. And it was full of dramatic surprises – such as sudden contrasts between soft and very loud.

An untidy page from one of Beethoven's notebooks

Whereas composing came very easily to Haydn and Mozart, Beethoven would struggle with a piece – crossing out, changing, improving it, until he was finally satisfied. He loved nature, and would take long walks in the country. He always carried a notebook in which he scribbled down any musical ideas which occurred to him. Later, tunes from these untidy pages would be altered time and again until he felt they were ready to be used. Beethoven became very careless of his appearance. During one of his country walks, he was arrested as a tramp and held by the police until his identity could be proved!

Before he was thirty, Beethoven was horrified to realise that he was becoming deaf. At first, he desperately tried to believe this was just a passing illness. But it gradually grew worse and, eventually, he became totally deaf.

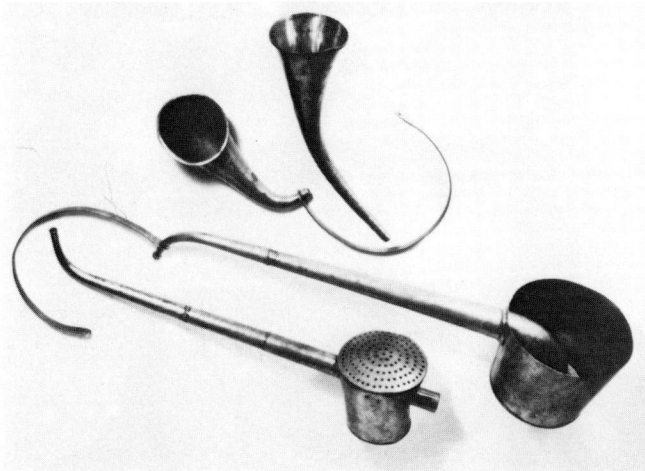

These are Beethoven's ear-trumpets, or hearing-aids

He had always been known for his rudeness and quick temper. Now, however, he quarrelled violently even with his closest friends. One day, a visitor found him pounding his piano in fury. Many of the strings had snapped due to Beethoven's desperate efforts to hear what he was composing. He was forced to give up playing and conducting at concerts. But Beethoven still continued to compose – now unable to hear his music except in his imagination.

First Movement from Piano Sonata No. 14 (the 'Moonlight' Sonata)

Beethoven composed 32 piano sonatas. A *sonata* is made up of three, sometimes four, separate pieces called 'movements'. Sonatas are usually for one or two instruments at the most – for instance, a piano; or perhaps a violin and piano.

Beethoven wrote the '*Moonlight*' Sonata in 1801. By that time, he already realised that he was becoming deaf. Most sonatas begin with a fairly quick movement, but Beethoven marks this first movement with the Italian word *adagio*, meaning 'slowly'. The title 'Moonlight' is not Beethoven's. The music took on this nickname when a critic said that this slow first movement made him think of moonlight shining on the Lake of Lucerne in Switzerland.

The music begins with gently rippling notes, smoothly grouped in threes. These soon become a hushed accompaniment to this melody:

This piano was presented to Beethoven by the London piano-maker, Thomas Broadwood

The violin

The violin has four strings. They are stretched across the bridge, and fixed to the tailpiece at one end and to the tuning pegs at the other.

To produce the sound, the violinist draws his bow across the strings. To make different notes, he must shorten the strings. He does this by pressing a string down against the finger board with his finger. The string can then only vibrate along the length from the bridge to the player's finger. The shorter the string, the higher the note will sound.

Instead of using the bow, the player may pluck the strings with his fingers. This is called *pizzicato*.

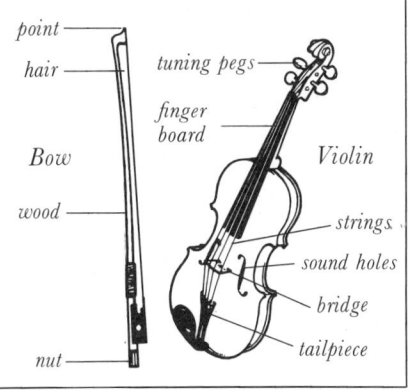

Third Movement from Violin Concerto in D major

In a *concerto*, a soloist (or sometimes, a group of soloists) is given rather difficult music to play, accompanied by an orchestra. A concerto is generally made up of three 'movements', or separate pieces:

1st movement: fairly fast
2nd movement: slower, and often song-like
3rd movement: swift, and usually light-hearted

Sometimes during a movement, the orchestra becomes silent while the soloist shows off his technique with some dazzling playing. A passage of music like this is called a *cadenza*.

The third movement of Beethoven's *Violin Concerto* is a lively *rondo*, in which the main tune comes round several times with different, contrasting, tunes played in between.

This is the main tune of Beethoven's Rondo:

You will also hear these two tunes which contrast with the main rondo tune:

This plan of the Rondo from Beethoven's *Violin Concerto* shows the order in which you will hear the three tunes **A**, **B** and **C**:

A¹	**B¹**	**A²**	**C**	**A³**	**B²**	**Cadenza**	**Coda**
the main rondo tune	first contrasting tune	main rondo tune again	second contrasting tune	main rondo tune again	first contrasting tune again	(violin alone)	('rounding off') built on Tune A

Symphony No. 6 in F major (the 'Pastoral' Symphony)

This, the sixth of Beethoven's 9 symphonies, shows his great love for the countryside. Most symphonies are made up of four movements, but this one has five.

Beethoven's *'Pastoral' Symphony* is an example of what we call *programme music* – music which tells a story, or paints a picture in sound. Here, there is no actual story – but in each of the five movements, the music in some way describes the sights and sounds of the countryside as they might appear to someone more used to living in a town or city.

Beethoven gives each of his five movements a descriptive title.

First movement: 'Awakening of happy feelings upon arriving in the countryside'
The Symphony opens quietly with this tune, played by violins:

Later, there is a second, more flowing, tune:

Then Beethoven builds up the rest of this first movement mainly using these two tunes – or just fragments taken from them (for instance, the tiny scrap of Tune **A** marked in the bracket).

Peasants merry-making in a painting by the Flemish artist, Pieter Brueghel

Violin

Second Movement: 'Scene by the Brook'
We know from one of Beethoven's notebooks that he actually spent quite some time beside a brook in the beautiful countryside not far from Vienna, jotting down ideas for this movement.

The music moves fairly slowly, but flows tunefully from the beginning to the end. Violins play the opening melody (**C**) while other instruments – two solo cellos in particular – suggest the peaceful rippling of the brook.

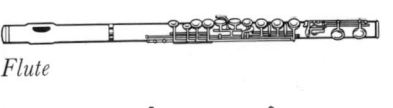

Flute

This movement of the Symphony is quite long. At the close, a flute, an oboe and two clarinets imitate the songs of a nightingale, a quail and a cuckoo.

Third Movement: 'Peasants' Merrymaking'
In this movement, Beethoven paints a musical picture of a group of peasants dancing and making merry after a hard day's work in the fields.

Strings begin a crisp, light introduction to this dance-tune:

The second tune (**E**), beginning off-the-beat, is played by the oboe. Now and then, the bassoon joins in with just a few notes – sounding rather drowsy, as if from drinking too much wine!

Oboe

Clarinet

The next section of music brings a sudden contrast: a louder, much more boisterous dance with two beats to each bar:

All these tunes come round again. Then we hear Tune **D** for the last time. The music grows louder and faster and rushes without a break into the fourth movement of the Symphony.

Fourth Movement: 'Thunderstorm'
A rumbling of distant thunder shudders on cellos
and double basses, and the pattering of the first
raindrops is heard on the violins:

Trumpet

Kettle drum

Horn

Trombone

Then the storm breaks with sudden fury. Brass
instruments and kettle drums add to the effect.
Jagged rhythms on violins and violas suggest
flashes of lightning, and rolls and crashes on
kettle drums imitate thunderclaps.

Eventually, the storm dies away. Woodwind
instruments paint blue skies, and the clear tone
of a solo flute leads the music straight into the
final movement of the Symphony.

*Fifth Movement: 'Shepherds' song. Happy and thankful
feelings after the storm'*
Beethoven designs this last movement as a
rondo, built upon this main tune – first hinted
at by clarinet and horn in turn, then played in
full by the violins:

This is how the famous French composer,
Hector Berlioz, described this final movement of
Beethoven's *'Pastoral'* Symphony:

'The Symphony ends with a hymn of
thanksgiving. Everything smiles. The shepherds
reappear, and answer each other on the
mountainside as they gather their scattered
flocks. The sky is serene. Calmness returns, and
we hear country songs and gentle melodies . . .'

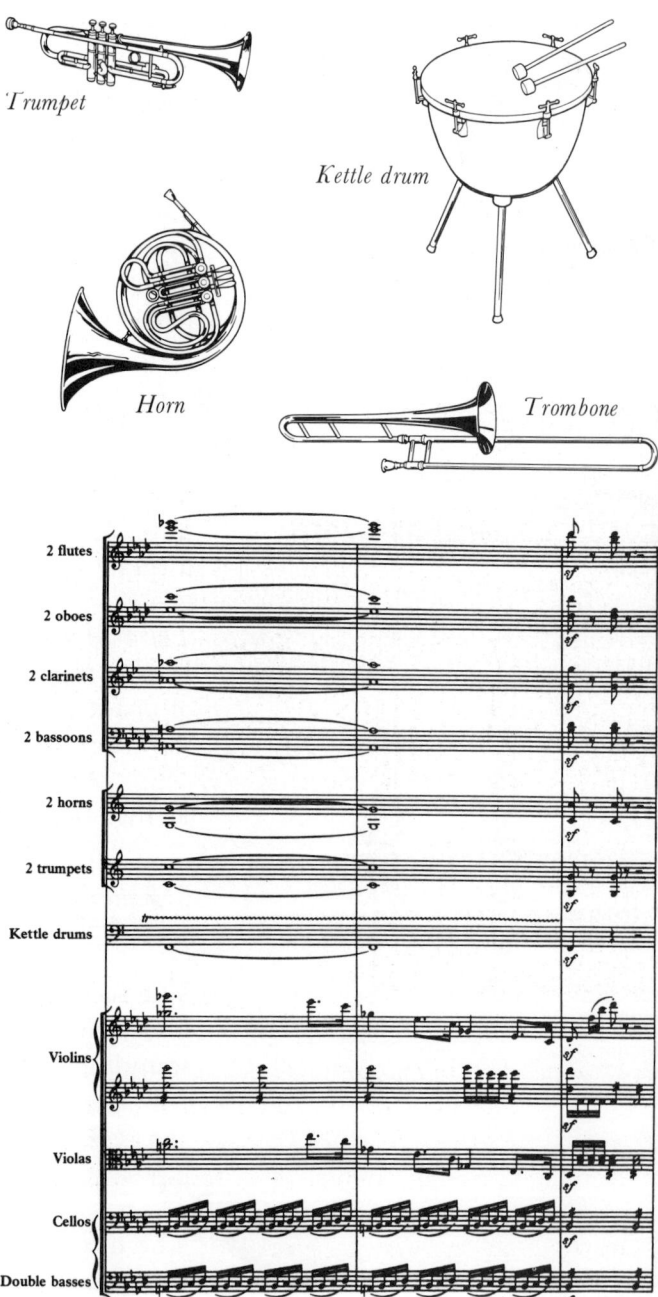

Above, you can see a page of the Storm music,
taken from the conductor's *orchestral score* – the
book containing the music played by all the
instruments. The instrumental 'parts' are printed
one below the other down the page, arranged
according to the four sections of the orchestra.

FRYDERYK CHOPIN

1810–1849 POLAND

Chopin's music quickly attracted attention. Besides performing at concerts, he was eagerly invited to play in the drawing-rooms of wealthy music-lovers. He made many friends – including the French painter, Delacroix, and the Hungarian composer and pianist, Franz Liszt.

Franz Liszt

Almost all Chopin's compositions are for piano alone. He received his first piano lessons from his sister at the age of four. He composed his first piece, a polonaise, when he was seven, and gave his first concert – playing a very difficult piano concerto – at the age of eight.

When he was twenty, Chopin left Poland – never to return. He took with him a small silver goblet filled with Polish earth, given to him by his friends. He travelled through Germany, giving concerts in several important cities. Then, a year later, he arrived in Paris. He was to make his home there for the rest of his life.

All his life, Chopin suffered from poor health. When he was twenty-eight, he became desperately ill with tuberculosis. He visited Majorca, hoping the climate there might improve his health. The inhabitants – afraid they too might catch the disease – demanded that he should leave the island. Instead, Chopin moved into a deserted monastery. Although he composed some of his finest pieces there, the chill and the dampness in the old building made his illness very much worse, and he was forced to return to Paris.

In 1848, Chopin visited England and Scotland. But loneliness – and the terror of knowing that he was dying – drove him back to Paris. He died there the following year. Earth from the silver goblet, brought with him from Poland eighteen years before, was sprinkled on his grave.

Polonaise No. 6 in A flat major, Opus 63

A *polonaise* is a Polish processional dance with three beats to a bar. The steps of a polonaise are very stately – almost 'walked' rather than danced. Yet the music itself is extremely rhythmic.

Although Chopin left Poland when he was twenty, never to return, his country was never far from his thoughts. In his Polonaises, he conjures up vivid musical pictures of the chivalry and pageantry of Poland's colourful history.

Chopin's *Polonaise in A flat major* begins with a dramatic introduction, which gradually builds up until it launches into this fiery main theme:

The mood of this music is proud and majestic. Now and then, the pianist plays a roaring scale passage which rushes angrily from almost the bottom to the top of the keyboard.

Later, listen for:
1. A brief tune (**B** below) which is accompanied by this typical polonaise rhythm:
2. The second appearance of the main theme (Tune **A**).
3. A section of music which begins with loud, spread chords. Then the left hand begins a rumbling *ostinato* (Italian for 'obstinately repeating'). Above this ostinato, rides Tune **C**.
4. The third, and last, appearance of Tune **A**, followed by an exciting *coda* to round off the piece.

Chopin often played this piano by the French maker, Erard

Etude in E major, Opus 10 No. 3

An *étude* is a 'study' – an often very difficult piece intended to improve a player's technique in some way. Chopin's 27 Etudes, however, are far more than just exercises for the pianist. 'Every one a poem!', wrote the German composer, Robert Schumann, when he first heard Chopin play them.

Chopin dedicated the first 12 of his Etudes to his friend, the famous Hungarian pianist and composer, Franz Liszt.

Chopin is often called 'the poet of the piano'. 'He really knows how to make the piano *sing*', wrote a critic – and this Etude begins with one of those smooth, singing melodies for which Chopin was so greatly admired (Tune **A**, below).

There is a change of mood in the middle section of the piece. The speed increases, and loud, pounding chords build up to a huge climax.

Then the tension relaxes, preparing the mood for the return of the peaceful opening melody.

Nocturne No. 2 in E flat major

A *nocturne* is a 'night-piece' – music whose mood matches ideas connected with night, such as calm, mystery and moonlight.

Chopin composed 21 Nocturnes. In these pieces, the pianist's left hand plays a smooth accompaniment while, above, the right hand sings a flowing melody. (It was exactly this kind of piece which earned Chopin the title: 'poet of the piano'.)

Beneath the main melody of the *Nocturne in E flat*, Chopin adds the words *dolce espressivo* – 'sweetly and expressively'. We hear this melody several times. Each time it is repeated, Chopin decorates it in a slightly different way.

From time to time he brings in another tune – very similar in mood to the main melody:

Only towards the end of the piece does the music become rather more forceful and dramatic. Then, after high trickling notes played by the right hand alone, the Nocturne ends in the same hushed mood as it began.

Waltz No. 7 in C sharp minor

A *waltz* (sometimes called by its French name, *valse*) is a lilting dance with three beats to a bar. However, unlike the orchestral ballroom variety by composers such as Johann Strauss, Chopin intended his Waltzes to be played and listened to, rather than danced.

Each of Chopin's Waltzes is made up of several sections of music which are contrasted in mood and speed. The pianist's right hand is often given very difficult notes to play, while his left hand provides a simple waltz accompaniment.

Chopin's *Waltz in C sharp minor* has three tunes. Tune **A**, in the minor key, is melancholy in mood and moves at a gentle speed:

Tune **B**, also in the minor key, is made up of patterns of swift, darting quavers:

Tune **C** is in the major key, and is slower and more wistful:

Chopin arranges his three waltz-tunes in this order:

A   B   C   B   A   B

Several of Chopin's piano pieces (including the *Waltz in C sharp minor*) have been arranged for orchestra to provide music for the ballet *Les Sylphides* – 'The Sylphs'. (In mythology, a sylph is a spirit of the air.) The setting of *Les Sylphides* is a wooded glade by moonlight.

GIUSEPPE VERDI

1813–1901   ITALY

Giuseppe Verdi is considered the greatest of all Italian opera composers. During his long life, he composed more than 30 operas, of which the best known are *Rigoletto*, *Il Trovatore*, *La Traviata*, and *Aida*.

Verdi was born the son of a village innkeeper, and even when he became world famous, he still remained a simple, honest peasant at heart. He bought a farm, spending as much time there as possible. He loved animals – especially dogs and horses. When away from home, he would send letters giving very detailed instructions about how they were to be fed and cared for.

Verdi had a flair for writing attractive tunes, and a sure instinct for building up vividly dramatic scenes in his operas. His characters are full-blooded, expressing their thoughts and feelings with powerful emotion. Verdi always considered the singers to be more important than the orchestra – but even so, he often supports the voices with exciting and strongly rhythmic orchestral accompaniments.

Il Trovatore (The Troubadour)

These are the main characters which take part in Verdi's opera, *Il Trovatore*:

The Count di Luna – a young nobleman of Aragon
Azucena – a gypsy woman
Manrico – the supposed son of Azucena, but really the brother of the Count
Leonora – lady-in-waiting to the Princess of Aragon

Act 1: The Duel

An important part of the story has already taken place before the opera begins. The Count di Luna's younger brother, as a baby, was said to have been cursed by an old gypsy woman. For this, she was burned as a witch. In revenge, her daughter, Azucena, stole the baby, intending to throw it into the same flames. But by a terrible mistake, she burned her own baby. She decided to bring up the stolen child as her son instead, calling him Manrico.

He, in fact, is the mysterious troubadour who has been serenading Leonora, lady-in-waiting to the Princess of Aragon. But the Count di Luna also loves Leonora – and challenges Manrico to a duel. (Both men are, of course, quite unaware that they are brothers.)

25

A dance in the gypsy camp

Act 2: The Gypsy

The scene is the gypsy camp on the mountainside. Dawn is breaking. The gypsies begin to work at their forges, swinging heavy hammers and crashing them down onto the anvils:

See how the first ray of day-light re-turn-ing   Who makes the gyp-sy's life of toil a life of plea-sure?

Manrico tells Azucena of his duel. How he disarmed the Count, yet was somehow compelled to spare his life. Manrico learns that Leonora, believing him dead, is about to become a nun.

The scene changes to a convent. The Count has come to seize Leonora – but Manrico arrives in time to prevent him.

Act 3: The Gypsy's Son

The Count lays siege to the castle where Manrico has taken Leonora. Soldiers capture Azucena as a spy. She is recognised as the gypsy who threw the Count's brother into the flames. Azucena denies this, but the Count holds her prisoner.

Manrico and Leonora are about to be married when news comes that Azucena is to be put to death by burning. Already, the glow of the flames can be seen from the window. As he leaves to rescue Azucena, Manrico swears vengeance on all who would do her harm.

Act 4: The Execution

Manrico has failed to rescue Azucena. He has been captured and imprisoned in a tower where both he and Azucena now await death. Leonora arrives. She has a plan to save Manrico. A death bell begins to toll, and voices are heard chanting the *Miserere* – a prayer for the dying. Leonora is overcome with dread:

The pray'r for the dy - ing in sol-emn de-vo - tion! I hear it a-round me, it fills me with dread!

Manrico's voice is heard distantly from the tower, urging death to come quickly:

Oh, from this life of tor - ment why is there no re - lease?

The Count appears. Leonora offers herself to him if he will set Manrico free. The Count agrees. But Leonora has poison hidden beneath the jewel in her ring. As she enters the tower to tell Manrico he is free, she swallows the poison – then dies in his arms. The Count, in fury, orders Manrico to be taken out, then forces Azucena to watch his execution. As Manrico dies, Azucena points to the Count and shrieks: 'He was your brother!'. And then: 'Mother – you are avenged at last!'.

The soldiers capture Azucena as a spy

JOHANN STRAUSS THE YOUNGER

1825–1899 AUSTRIA

It is impossible to hear the name Strauss mentioned without thinking of Viennese dance music – especially the waltz, with its lilting, three-beats-to-a-bar rhythm.

Johann Strauss the Younger composed his first waltz when he was only six years old. His father – Johann the Elder, who was famous in Vienna as both composer and conductor – tried to discourage him from becoming a musician. But the boy took violin and composition lessons in secret and, at the age of nineteen, got together an orchestra of his own, playing music composed by his father and himself.

Five years later, when his father died, he joined their two orchestras together. He gave concerts throughout Europe and the United States, and was enthusiastically welcomed wherever he appeared as the leading composer and conductor of Viennese dance music.

The opening bars of 'The Blue Danube Waltz'

Johann Strauss the Younger composed almost 200 waltzes. Among them, are *Tales from the Vienna Woods*, which includes a haunting zither solo; *The Emperor Waltz*, beginning with two beats to a bar instead of three; and – most famous of all – *The Blue Danube*. Then there are other dances popular in Vienna at the time, such as mazurkas, galops and polkas.

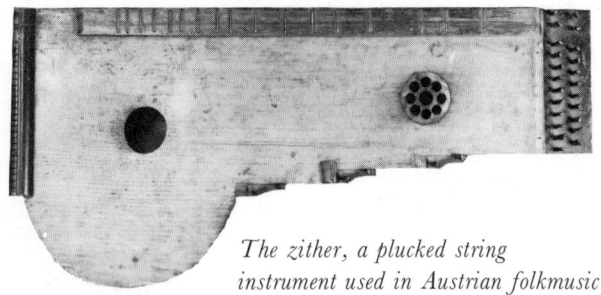

The zither, a plucked string instrument used in Austrian folkmusic

Johann also wrote several operettas (operas in a rather lighter style, in which the dialogue is spoken rather than sung). The best known of these is *Die Fledermaus* ('The Bat').

Each year, on New Year's Day, a special concert of music by the Strauss family takes place in Vienna. You may not be lucky enough to attend one of these concerts – but they are shown each year on television.

The Blue Danube Waltz

A waltz has three beats to a bar – usually in a '*dum*-dah-dah' kind of rhythm. When it was first danced in the elegant ballrooms of Vienna, at the end of the 18th century, a few people were shocked (the waltz was one of the first dances in which the partners held each other closely). But most people were captivated by the gaiety and lightness of its whirling movements and the 'waltz craze' soon swept right across Europe.

The Blue Danube must be the most famous waltz ever written. Like most waltzes by Strauss, this piece is really a whole *chain* of waltzes, each containing two tunes.

First, a slow, shimmering introduction in which horns mysteriously hint at the famous main theme (to be heard later as Tune **1A**). Then follows the chain of five contrasting dances with tunes that are joyful and lilting (**1A** and **3A**), broad and flowing (**4A**), and sometimes vigorous and strongly rhythmic (**5B**). Strauss's orchestration is varied and colourful – and you will often hear the snare drum bringing a crispness to the rhythms.

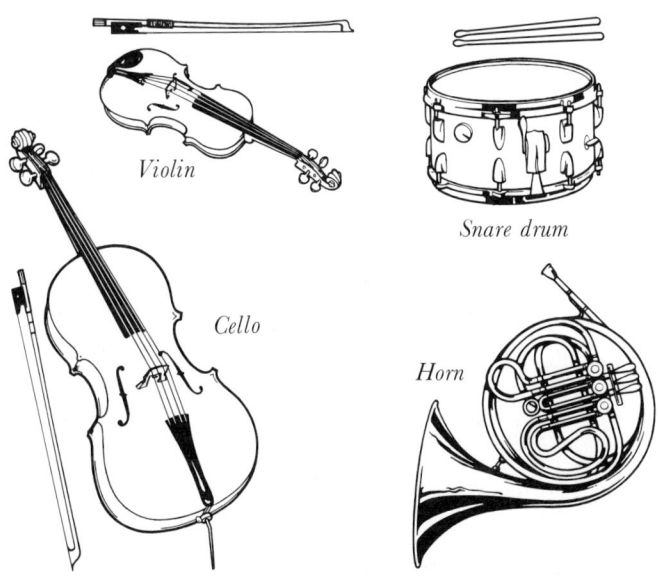

Violin

Snare drum

Cello

Horn

After the fifth waltz, Strauss reminds us of three of the tunes we have heard: **2A**, **4A** and **1A**. Then there is a sudden pause – followed by a *coda* (Italian for 'tail', or 'rounding-off'). This begins dreamily; but finally, the music sweeps to a breathless, whirling conclusion.

Here is a snatch of each of the ten tunes which make up this chain of five waltzes:

Pizzicato Polka

Johann Strauss the Younger had two brothers, Josef and Eduard, who also became composers. Johann and Josef both shared in composing this *Pizzicato Polka*. They gave it this title because, during the entire piece, the string instruments are played *pizzicato* (or plucked). Johann and Josef scored the music for strings alone – but it is sometimes heard in a version in which the strings are joined by woodwind and percussion instruments in the middle of the piece.

Pizzicato Polka is built up in three main sections. A plan of the music looks like this:

Section 1 A B A	Section 2 C D	Section 3 A B A	Coda

Notice that there are two tunes in each section but that the music of Section 3 is the same as that of Section 1. The piece is rounded off by a coda, during which the speed increases to make an exciting ending to the music.

These are the four tunes that you will hear:

The dance known as the polka was originally a folk dance from Czechoslovakia (or Bohemia, as it was then known). It takes its name from the Czech word *pulka*, meaning 'half', and the story goes that it was invented by a servant girl who was forced to take rather short steps as she made up the dance, due to the lack of space in her tiny attic room. Later, the polka was taken into the glittering ballrooms of Vienna, where it became almost as popular as the waltz.

Dancing in Vienna during the ball season

Violin

Viola

Cello

Double bass

EDVARD GRIEG

1843–1907 NORWAY

Grieg's mother was able to trace her family back to the Vikings. His father's ancestors had originally come from Scotland to settle in Norway after the Battle of Culloden in 1746.

Grieg took a keen interest in his country's folk music. In many of his pieces, he included Norwegian folk melodies or the rhythms of Norwegian folk dances. The freshness of his music appealed to many people, and he soon became known in other countries besides Norway.

Yet in spite of his fame, Grieg remained a shy man who liked nothing better than to live quietly at his house in the countryside near Bergen. He called his home Troldhaugen, which means 'Hill of the Trolls'. (A troll is a kind of dwarf, often found in Norwegian folk tales.)

In the grounds at Troldhaugen, Grieg built a hut – just large enough to take a piano, a chair and writing table, and a stove. Here, overlooking the beautiful Hardanger Fjord, he was able to write his music in complete peace.

Grieg's house, which he called 'Troldhaugen'

Two pieces from 'Peer Gynt'

In 1874, Norway's most famous playwright, Henrik Ibsen, decided to make a stage version of his long dramatic poem called *Peer Gynt*. He asked Grieg to compose some incidental music – pieces to introduce certain scenes, accompany some of the stage action, and to entertain the audience during scene-changes. Included in the music which Grieg composed for *Peer Gynt* are several of his best-loved pieces.

The hero of the play – Peer Gynt himself – is a selfish, headstrong, yet likeable character. Arriving uninvited at a wedding, he carries off the bride, Ingrid. For this, he is immediately branded as an outlaw – to be shot on sight.

Peer soon grows tired of Ingrid and leaves her. He decides to explore the caves deep beneath the mountains. This is the dark kingdom of the hideous trolls. They capture Peer and make him their prisoner, but fortunately he manages to escape.

Peer builds a hut for himself, high on the mountainside. Here, he is joined by Solveig, a girl from the village. Because of her love for Peer, she has left family and friends to be with him. But Peer, realising that he is not worthy of her love, decides to seek his fortune far away from Norway. He has many adventures but all his plans end in failure, and he is never able to find true happiness.

Eventually, an older if not wiser man, Peer decides to return home to Norway, experiencing storm and shipwreck on the way. When at last he arrives at the village where he was born, he finds that no one recognises him. No one even remembers the brave Peer Gynt.

He leaves the village and begins to climb the mountain. He meets a tall man, dressed all in black. As they talk, Peer realises it is the Devil in disguise. He has come to claim Peer's soul. In despair, Peer looks about him. He sees a hut, long forgotten on the mountain slope. The door opens – and Solveig, now old and blind, appears in the glow shed by the lamp. She recognises Peer's voice, and welcomes him with tears of joy. Peer's soul is saved – for the present – by the strength of her courage and her love.

Morning

This piece was really intended to introduce a scene showing Peer's adventures in North Africa. But Grieg's music sounds as cool and fresh as a spring morning in the mountains of Norway.

This melody is first played alternately by flute and oboe:

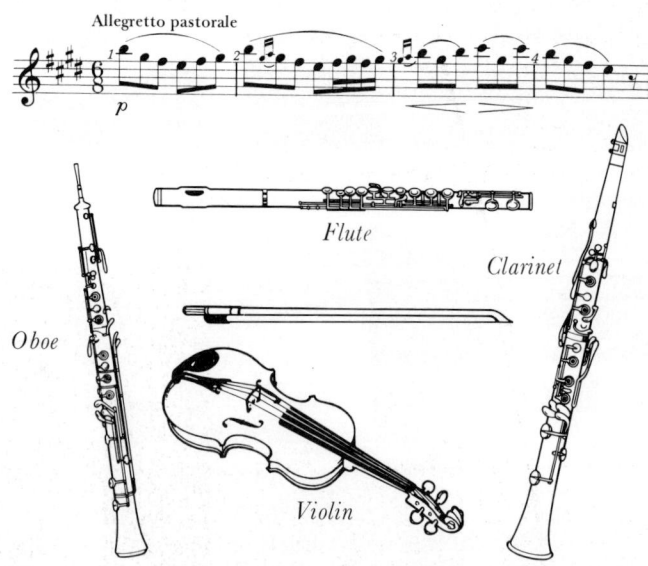

Flute

Clarinet

Oboe

Violin

Then we hear richer sounds from the strings – as if the rising sun suddenly bathes the landscape in its golden warmth.

Towards the end of the piece, woodwind instruments seem to suggest the songs of birds.

In the Hall of the Mountain King

This rather frightening, but exciting, music is from the scene in the play when Peer explores the dark caves beneath the mountains. This is the kingdom of the hideous trolls and their ruler, the Mountain King.

In the gloom, Peer becomes aware of shufflings and scrabblings as weird shapes begin to creep towards him from dark, shadowy corners. With horror, he realises that he is being surrounded by the trolls. Very slowly, they close in. . . . Then suddenly, they attack – pinching, biting, scratching. Desperately, Peer struggles to free himself. But he is dragged forward, and thrown down at the feet of the evil Mountain King. . . .

For this music, Grieg uses only one tune which is played eighteen times. The piece begins very softly and stealthily – and here, the bassoon plays an important part. Then the music grows gradually faster and louder, building up to a terrifying climax.

Alla marcia (in march style)

The bassoon

This is the deepest-sounding of the four main woodwind instruments. Its tube is more than 8 feet long, and so it is folded back on itself to make it more easy to manage.

The bassoon, like the oboe, has a double reed. This is fitted into the end of the crook (given this name, as you can see, because it looks like a shepherd's crook).

The bassoon can sound smooth and rather sad. But when it is asked to play *staccato* (making the notes sound crisp and short), it can either chortle along with good humour or – as in this piece by Grieg – sound gruff, and perhaps menacing.

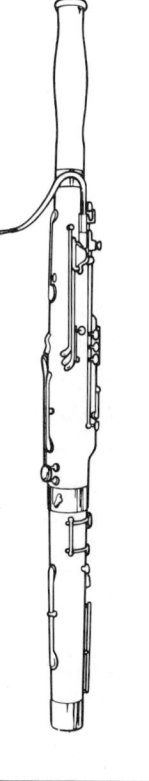

In the Hall of the evil Mountain King

EDWARD ELGAR

1857–1934 ENGLAND

Most composers study music at a college or university. Elgar taught himself – learning as he went along by playing and composing.

His father, besides being a church organist, kept a music shop in Worcester, and it was here that Elgar picked up a good deal of his musical knowledge. He taught himself to play several of the instruments in the shop, especially the violin and the bassoon. He became violinist in several small orchestras, and played bassoon in a local woodwind group. Sometimes he conducted as well. Many of his experiences at first hand, both as player and conductor, gave him a superb understanding of orchestration – the special technique of writing for full orchestra.

He began to compose in earnest, and had several orchestral and choral pieces performed, not only in Worcester, but in London as well. But it was not until the first performance of his 'Enigma' Variations in 1899 that Elgar gained true recognition. People then began to realise that – for the first time for two centuries – England had a composer of worldwide importance.

The Malvern Hills

Variations 9 and 11 from 'Enigma' Variations

When a composer writes a set of variations, he takes a tune (which he calls the 'theme') and presents it over and over again, but always disguising it – or *varying* it – in different, interesting ways. He may take as his theme a tune that is already well known, or he may think up one of his own.

Elgar composed his *'Enigma' Variations* while he was living in Malvern. He dedicated the music 'to my friends pictured within'. And in fact, each variation is a musical portrait of one of these friends. Included are Elgar's wife, a pianist, a friend keen on amateur dramatics, a viola player, an architect (who built Elgar's house in Malvern), a music publisher, and an organist who owned a particularly lively bulldog. The last variation of all is a musical portrait of the composer himself.

Enigma means 'a puzzle', and the puzzle here is to do with the theme on which Elgar bases his variations. He mysteriously remarked that right through the music 'another, larger theme 'goes' – but is not played'. What this other, unheard tune actually is, no one has ever discovered, but many have tried to guess. (*God Save the Queen* and *Auld Lang Syne* have both been suggested.) However, this is the theme we *do* hear before the variations begin:

The theme is in *ternary* (three-part) form: **ABA**. **A** is played both times by violins, and is in a minor key. That, together with the effect of falling notes in each phrase, and a rest at the beginning of each bar, makes the music sound sad and hesitating. **B** presents a musical contrast. It is in the brighter-sounding major key, and is first given to woodwind instruments.

Variation 9 ('Nimrod')
Nimrod is the mighty hunter mentioned in the Bible. And this was Elgar's nickname for a friend of his, a music publisher named August Jaeger – the joke here being that in the German language, the word *jaeger* means 'a hunter'. This variation begins very softly on strings alone. Later, the music builds up to a huge climax – then, quite suddenly, dies away.

Elgar varies his original theme here by arranging it in three beats to a bar instead of four, and by putting it into the major key. But there is still a very strong likeness – match bars 1 to 4 of this variation against the same bars of the original theme.

Variation 11 ('G.R.S.')
These initials stand for George Robertson Sinclair, organist of Hereford Cathedral. But this music was really suggested by his bulldog, Dan, tumbling into the River Wye (bar 1), swimming earnestly for the bank (bars 2 and 3), then scrambling out with a joyful bark (bar 5). If you compare this music with the original theme, you will find that bars 2 and 3 are **A** in disguise. And that bar 4 is a very much quicker version of the first bar of **B**.

Pomp and Circumstance March No. 1 in D major

Elgar composed five marches which he called *Pomp and Circumstance*. When someone asked why an important composer should spend time writing marches, Elgar replied: 'I know that a lot of people like to celebrate events with music. To these people, I have given tunes.'

The most popular of these marches is the first. This brings in the tune to which the words 'Land of Hope and Glory' are often sung. Elgar became excited as he wrote this music, saying: 'I've got a tune that will knock 'em flat! A tune like that comes once in a lifetime.'

This is how Elgar builds up his march:
1. First a short, very fiery, introduction.
2. The first main tune (Tune **A**, below) is brisk and has a very lively rhythm.
3. The second tune (**B**) is broader, and more flowing. It is first played *piano* (softly) by the strings. Then *forte* (loudly), with brass and percussion instruments joining in.
4. The lively first tune returns.
5. The broad second tune (**B**) comes round again, with drums and cymbals to mark each beat.
6. Then Elgar brings his music to an exciting, sparkling conclusion.

Elgar's *Pomp and Circumstance March No. 1* is played at the last night of the Promenade Concerts in London each summer. Everyone joins in by singing these words:

> 'Land of Hope and Glory,
> Mother of the free,
> How shall we extol thee
> Who are born of thee?
> Wider still and wider
> Shall thy bounds be set.
> God who made thee mighty,
> Make thee mightier yet!'

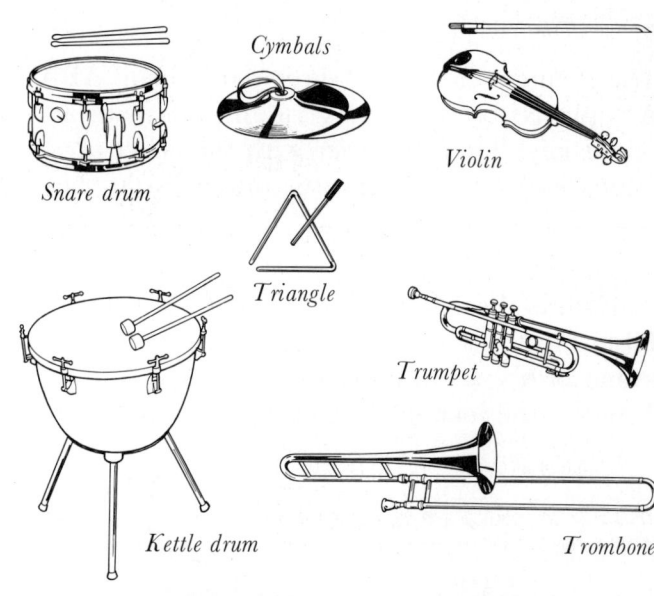

Cymbals

Violin

Snare drum

Triangle

Trumpet

Kettle drum

Trombone

ALBÉNIZ

  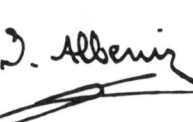

The early life of Isaac Albéniz reads like an incredible adventure story! As a pianist, he gave his first concert at the age of four. At seven, he played in Paris, and then took the entrance examination to become a student at the famous Conservatoire, or music college.

He played brilliantly, but amusing himself while waiting for the professors' decision, he sent a ball crashing through one of the Conservatoire's magnificent windows. He failed the examination – the official reason being that he was too young. So instead, he studied music in Madrid.

By now, he had begun to compose, and had heard a Spanish dance of his, called Paso Doblé, played by a military band in Barcelona.

When he was nine, Albéniz ran away from home, deciding to earn money from his piano playing. Apparently, one of his stunts at this time – which must have astounded his audiences – was to play sitting with his back to the piano!

Somehow, the boy managed to give concerts in several Spanish towns before a local mayor firmly put him on a train for home. But this did not suit him at all. He changed trains, went elsewhere, and gave more concerts. When robbers stole all the money he had earned, he simply made his mind up to earn more.

When he was twelve, Albéniz decided to try his luck abroad. He became a stowaway on board a liner bound for South America. He was discovered – but passengers and crew alike made a great fuss of him, and he was eventually allowed to land.

Incredibly, he gave concerts in Argentina, Uruguay, Brazil, Cuba, and Puerto Rico. Then he toured the United States from San Francisco to New York. At the age of fourteen, he decided to make for home – but stopped on the way to play at concerts in Liverpool and London.

Back in Europe, Albéniz took more piano lessons and composed a vast amount of music. Then, at eighteen, he achieved his greatest ambition – he went to Budapest to take lessons from the famous Hungarian pianist and composer, Franz Liszt.

Most of Albéniz's compositions are for piano. In many of them, we hear the rhythms of Spanish folk dances, and are often reminded of sounds of Spanish instruments such as the guitar and castanets.

Seguidillas (Castillian Dance)

Castille is a region of northern Spain. A *seguidillas* is really for both dancing and singing. Sung sections, called *coplas*, alternate with lively dance sections in a more definite rhythm. In a true *seguidillas*, guitar and castanets are used as an accompaniment.

Albéniz writes his piece for piano solo – but even so, in the dance sections there is a strong suggestion of the crisp clicking of castanets and the twang of guitar strings.

Castanets

A short introduction sets the rhythm going – then the dance begins:

This is the slightly slower tune of the *coplas*:

The countryside in Castille

A lively Spanish dance accompanied by guitar and castanets

Tango in D, from the Suite 'España' (Spain)

The modern ballroom dance known as the *tango* is Argentinian rather than Spanish – but originally, this dance came from the region of southern Spain called Andalusia.

A *tango* has two beats to a bar, and you will often hear this kind of rhythm:

Albéniz's *Tango in D* is the best known of all his compositions. Although he wrote this music for piano, it has been arranged for guitar by the great Spanish guitarist, Andrés Segovia.

Here is the rather wistful tune of Albéniz's *Tango*:

The guitar

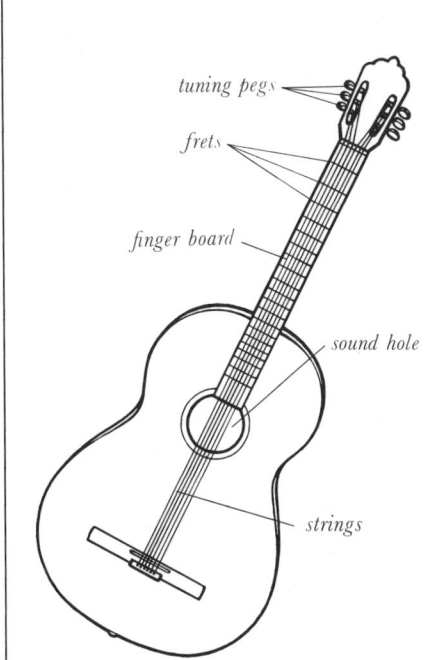

The guitar is usually thought of as being a typically Spanish instrument – but nowadays, it is played in every country in the world. It is sometimes called the Spanish, or 'acoustic', guitar to distinguish it from the more modern electric guitar.

The six strings are stretched across a flat, hollow body, shaped like a figure 8. Each string is fixed to a tuning peg which can be tightened or slackened to adjust the pitch. The strings are plucked with the fingers of the right hand, or with a *plectrum* made of some kind of hard material.

On the fingerboard are thin strips of metal called *frets*. These show the player where to find the different notes by pressing down the strings with the fingers of the left hand.

The six strings are tuned to these notes:

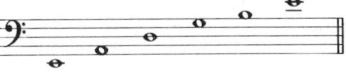

El Corpus en Sevilla (Easter Festival in Seville)

This comes from a set of piano pieces which Albéniz called *Iberia* – an old name for Spain. These pieces, which are considered to be Albéniz's best work, present twelve musical pictures of different parts of Spain. The style of piano-writing in these pieces reminds us that, for a while, Albéniz took lessons from Liszt. All twelve pieces are extremely difficult for the pianist – so difficult, in fact, that Albéniz himself found them almost unplayable, and nearly decided to burn them! The last piece in the set was completed in the year in which Albéniz died. A few years later, a friend of his – a Spanish conductor named Fernandez Arbós – arranged several of the pieces for full orchestra. *El Corpus en Sevilla* paints a vivid picture of an Easter Festival in the streets of Seville in southern Spain.

This is how Albéniz builds up his music:
1. The crisp rhythm of a joyful march – quietly at first, as if a colourful procession is approaching from the distance:

Flute

2. The music becomes more flowing as a broad melody (**E**, below) is played loudly by the brass, above crashing drums and cymbals. Tubular bells suggest the triumphant pealing of all the church bells of Seville.

3. A slower, more peaceful section, in which the cor anglais (a large kind of oboe with a deeper voice) sings a melody which at first is very similar to Tune **E**.
4. The march music returns. It is interrupted by tune **E**, then continues on its way, gaining in speed and excitement.
5. The rhythm changes from two beats in a bar to three – and the march is transformed into a joyful, whirling dance.
6. A silence. Then the piece ends with slow, rather hushed music – as if night has fallen, and the festival is over.

Trumpet

Cor anglais

SERGEY PROKOFIEV

1891–1953   U.S.S.R.

Prokofiev was writing his first piano pieces when he was five, and composed a short opera when he was eight. At thirteen, he became a student at the Conservatoire in St. Petersburg (the city now known as Leningrad). One of his teachers was the famous Russian composer, Rimsky-Korsakov. By the time Prokofiev had completed his musical studies, he had already made a name as a composer and pianist.

Prokofiev left Russia at the time of the Russian Revolution. He travelled the world, passing through Siberia, Japan and Honolulu, and stayed for two years in America. Then he settled in Paris. Much of his music at that time did not greatly attract people. It was very rhythmic, and colourfully orchestrated – but audiences complained that it sounded too harsh and that Prokofiev could not write a good tune. In 1932, he returned to Russia, and the music he composed then (which includes *Peter and the Wolf* and the ballet *Romeo and Juliet*) is much more mellow and tuneful.

Third Movement from Symphony No. 1 in D major (the 'Classical')

Prokofiev was twenty-five when he composed his first symphony. He called it the 'Classical' because he deliberately set out to make the music sound similar in style to symphonies by Classical composers such as Haydn and Mozart. Prokofiev uses an orchestra of the same size, and the rhythms of the music have a similar grace and elegance. But he frequently takes a tune and gives it a sudden twist, sending it into an unexpected key. This gives the music a flavour which is very definitely of the 20th century.

The third movement of Prokofiev's *'Classical' Symphony* is a *gavotte* – a very dignified dance which was popular during the 18th century. Prokofiev shapes this movement in *ternary* form:
Tune **A** – Tune **B** – Tune **A** again.

Prokofiev

Peter and the Wolf – A Musical Tale for Children

In *Peter and the Wolf,* Prokofiev presents a story in both words and music. Each character taking part is represented by one or more instruments of the orchestra – rather like the actors in a play. So as we listen to the story, we come to recognise the special sounds of these different instruments. Before the story begins, Prokofiev introduces us to the characters, one by one.

The high, chirruping music of the Bird is played by the flute:

Flute

The melancholy tune of the Duck is played by the oboe:

Oboe

The stealthy, stalking tune of the Cat is played by the clarinet – in its lower register, where the notes sound dark and velvety rich:

Clarinet

The tune of Peter's rather grumpy old Grandfather is played, low down in the bass, by the bassoon:

Bassoon

42

The Wolf's music is played by three horns:

Peter – the brave young hero of the story – is represented by all the string instruments of the orchestra. This is Peter's tune:

Horns

Violin

Viola

Double bass

Cello

Later in the story, we hear the gunshots of the Hunters crashing out on the kettle drums and the big, bass drum:

Bass drum

Kettle drums

Once we have been introduced to these instruments and their tunes, Prokofiev unfolds his story in words and music.

AARON COPLAND

Born 1900 U.S.A.

A.Copland

Aaron Copland, America's most important 20th century composer, was born in Brooklyn, New York. He first studied music in New York and then, for three years, in France. Returning to America in 1924, Copland had very clear ideas about the kind of music he wanted to compose:

> 'When I returned to New York after my musical studies in Europe, I definitely set out to write music which everyone could understand was American.'

Copland brings an American flavour to many of his pieces by using rhythms borrowed from jazz, and by including American folksongs. This is especially true of three ballets he has written called *Billy the Kid*, *Rodeo*, and *Appalachian Spring*.

Suite from the ballet: 'Billy the Kid'

Billy the Kid (real name – William H. Bonney) lived from 1859 to 1881. He was born in New York but, as a boy, joined a group of pioneers making the trek to the West.

For a time, Billy lived in Silver City, New Mexico. By the age of eighteen, he was leader of a gang of cattle rustlers – and was already wanted for murder.

Billy's very brief but violent career as an outlawed bandit and killer quickly made him into one of the fabulous legends of the American Southwest. Countless stories – many of them untrue – were told of his crimes and adventures. He was said to have notches on his pistol boasting of twenty-one killings. And though he was captured many times, he always managed to escape – until, at the age of twenty-two, he met his death at the hands of Pat Garrett, Sheriff of Lincoln County, and Billy's one-time friend.

Billy the Kid

REWARD
($5,000.00)

Reward for the capture, dead or alive,
of one Wm. Wright, better known as
"BILLY THE KID"

Age, 18. Height, 5 feet, 3 inches.
Weight, 125 lbs. Light hair, blue
eyes and even features. He is
the leader of the worst band of
desperadoes the Territory has
ever had to deal with. The above
reward will be paid for his capture
or positive proof of his death.
JIM DALTON, Sheriff.

DEAD OR ALIVE!
"BILLY THE KID"

Here is Copland's own description of the story of his ballet, *Billy the Kid*:

'The action begins and closes on the open prairie. The central portion of the ballet concerns itself with the significant moments in the life of Billy the Kid.

The first scene is a street in a frontier town. Familiar figures amble by. Cowboys saunter into town, some on horseback, others with their lassoes. Some Mexican women dance a *jarabe* which is interrupted by a fight between two drunks. Attracted by the gathering crowd, Billy is seen for the first time as a boy of twelve with his mother. The brawl turns ugly, guns are drawn, and in some unaccountable way, Billy's mother is killed. Without an instant's hesitation, in cold fury, Billy draws a knife from a cowhand's sheath and stabs his mother's slayers. His short but famous career has begun.

In swift succession, we see episodes from Billy's later life. At night, under the stars, in a quiet card game with his outlaw friends. Hunted by a posse led by his former friend, Pat Garrett, Billy is pursued. A running battle ensues. Billy is captured. A drunken celebration takes place. Billy in prison is, of course, followed by one of Billy's legendary escapes.

Tired and worn in the desert, Billy rests with his girl. Starting from a deep sleep, he senses movement in the shadows. The posse has finally caught up with him. It is the end.'

In the music for his ballet, *Billy the Kid*, Copland uses several American cowboy songs, including 'Great Grandad', 'Old Paint', 'The Old Chisholm Trail', 'The Dying Cowboy' and 'Riding Free'.

As you will hear, these songs do not appear note for note. Copland often alters the rhythm of the tunes, and even the melody-notes themselves. 'I can't imagine Billy without these cowboy tunes,' says Copland. 'Of course, what I hoped to do was to give these tunes my own flavour.'

Copland's ballet was very successful. Later, he selected some of the music to make a *suite*. This does not cover the entire story of the ballet, but brings together seven sections of the music:

1. The Open Prairie

This music creates a fresh, outdoor atmosphere. Copland builds up a musical picture of the vast, open spaces of the prairie lands in the Southwest of America.

2. Street in a Frontier Town

Here are some of the tunes which Copland uses in this quite lengthy second section of his Suite:

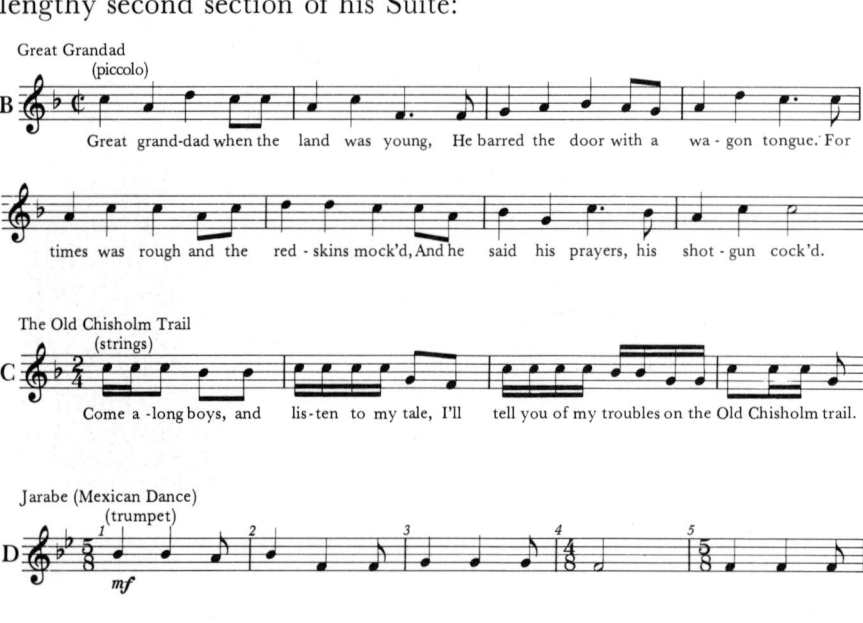

('Paint' comes from the Spanish, *pinto*, meaning horse.)

3. Card Game at Night (Prairie Night)

Soft, peaceful night-music. Flute and violins are the main instruments. Later, there is a solo for trumpet.

4. Gun Battle

A running battle which ends in Billy's capture. Wild, jagged rhythms on percussion instruments and harsh chords for the brass.

5. Celebration after Billy's Capture

Gay, jaunty music – colourful sounds from wind and percussion.

Riding Free

Rid - ing free. Rid - ing free. There's a price on his head and he's rid - ing free. But the sher - iff with his gun hunts a kil - ler on the run and soon he'll shoot him dead. There's a price on Bil - ly's head and soon they'll shoot him dead!

6. Billy's Death

A quiet lament, played mainly by the string section of the orchestra.

7. The Open Prairie

A return to the music of the opening section, Tune **A**, which builds up to a menacing climax on the full orchestra.

Variations on a Shaker song, from the ballet 'Appalachian Spring'

The story of this ballet takes place in the hills of Pennsylvania during the 19th century. It tells of a group of settlers who hold a celebration in springtime around a newly-built farmhouse. The two main characters in the ballet are a young farmer and the girl who shortly becomes his bride.

About three-quarters of the way through the ballet, Copland writes five variations on a song borrowed from the Shaker religion, called 'Simple Gifts'. As these variations are played, the newly-married couple are shown carrying out daily tasks on their new farm. The Shaker tune is first played by a solo clarinet:

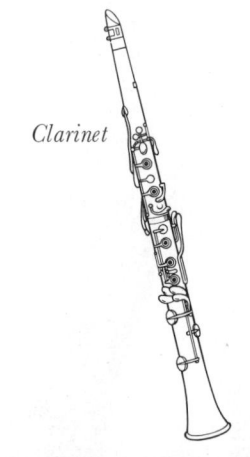

Clarinet

This is what happens to the tune in the variations:
1. The tune is played slightly faster by oboe and bassoon.
2. The first half of the tune only, twice as slowly, on violas and trombones. Violins and horns come in with the tune later.
3. A very lively variation for trumpets and trombones against swift, scurrying passages for violins and violas.
4. The second half of the tune only, flowing, on the woodwind.
5. For the full orchestra – broadly, and triumphantly. The tune rides proudly above rich, striding chords, and each main beat is punched out strongly on the drums.

Lives of the Composers

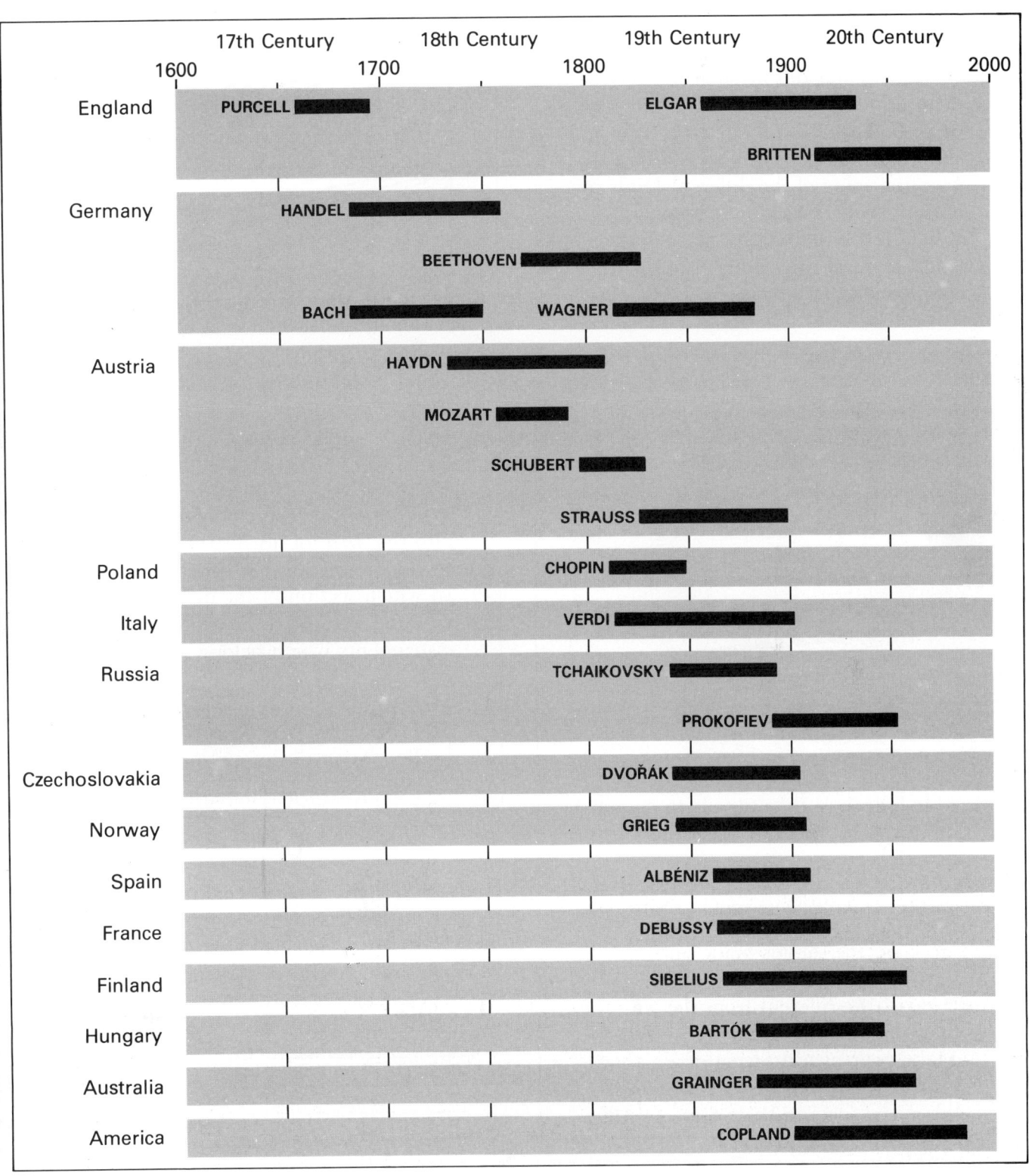

17th Century | 18th Century | 19th Century | 20th Century

1600 · 1700 · 1800 · 1900 · 2000

England — PURCELL, ELGAR, BRITTEN

Germany — HANDEL, BEETHOVEN, BACH, WAGNER

Austria — HAYDN, MOZART, SCHUBERT, STRAUSS

Poland — CHOPIN

Italy — VERDI

Russia — TCHAIKOVSKY, PROKOFIEV

Czechoslovakia — DVOŘÁK

Norway — GRIEG

Spain — ALBÉNIZ

France — DEBUSSY

Finland — SIBELIUS

Hungary — BARTÓK

Australia — GRAINGER

America — COPLAND

HENRY PURCELL

A.

a) In which century did Purcell live?

b) In which choir did he sing as a boy?

c) What kind of job did he take when his voice broke?

d) Where did he become organist in 1679?

e) Mention some of the different kinds of music which Purcell composed.

f) Where is Purcell buried?

g) Can you name any other English composers?

B.

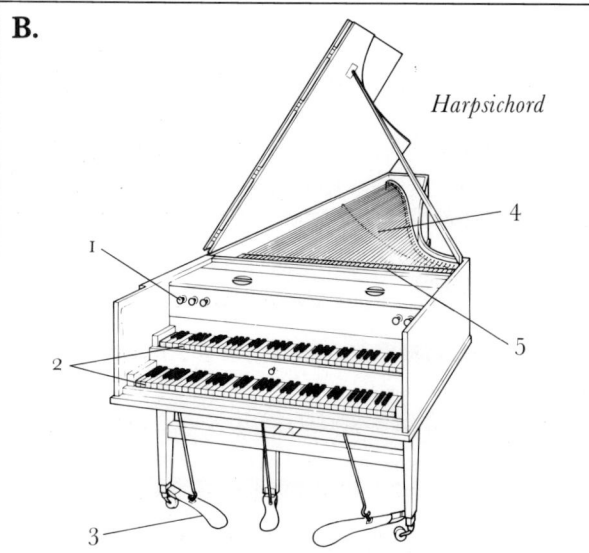

Harpsichord

a) Match each of these words to one of the numbers on the drawing of the harpsichord.

| strings | pedals | manuals | stops | jacks |

b) How are the sounds made on the harpsichord?

c) How is this different from the way the piano makes its sound?

d) Make your own drawing of a harpsichord – but instead of numbers for the parts, write in their correct names.

C.

a) Which of these trumpets is a modern trumpet, and which is of the kind used in Purcell's time?

b) What is the main difference between these two kinds of trumpet?

c) How would a trumpeter of Purcell's time have made the different notes sound on his instrument?

d) What does a trumpeter sometimes fit into the 'bell' of his instrument, in order to change the kind of sound it makes?

e) In which section of the orchestra would you find trumpets? Name other instruments which belong to the same section.

f) Make a drawing of a modern trumpet. Add these words, with arrows pointing to the correct places on your drawing:

| valves | bell | mouthpiece |

D. Each of these puzzles contains *two* musical words. In each puzzle, fill in the missing letters which will complete the first word and also begin the second word.

1. | P | U | R | | | | O |

2. | O | R | G | | T | H | E | M |

3. | P | L | E | C | | | | P | E | T |

GEORGE FRIDERIC HANDEL

A. Make a copy of this framework. Then, using the clues given below, see if you can fill in the missing words.

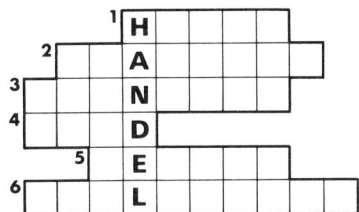

1. German town where Handel was born.
2. Music for singers and orchestra, usually presenting a story from the Bible – but there is no acting, just singing.
3. A lively dance, associated with sailors.
4. Very important to the sound of an oboe.
5. Christian name both of Handel and his employer who later became King of England.
6. Best known chorus from Handel's *Messiah*.

B.

Oboe

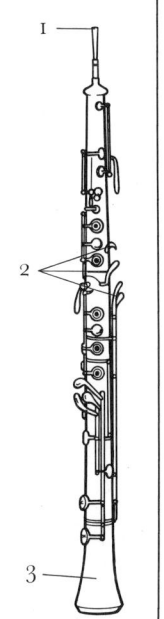

a) Match each of these words to one of the numbers on the drawing of the oboe:

keys	reed	bell

b) Does the oboe have a single reed, or a double reed?
c) To which of the four sections of the orchestra does the oboe belong?
d) Name two more instruments from the same section of the orchestra.
e) Make your own drawing of an oboe – but instead of numbers, write in the correct name for each part.

C.

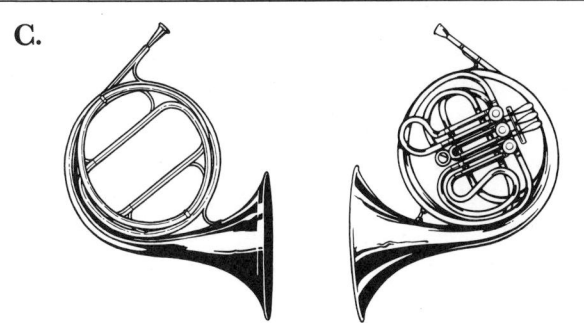

a) Which of these is a modern horn, and which is of the kind used in Handel's day?
b) Which of these horns has valves, and which has only crooks? What are crooks?
c) Which of these two horns do you think could play more notes?

D. *Air* from the *Water Music* by Handel

Handel's title really means 'song'. From the beginning to the end of this piece, Handel's melody flows with a steady, graceful rhythm.

You will hear these eight bars of melody played several times during this *Air*:

a) On one occasion when these eight bars are played by the violins, another instrument plays a long-held note, high above. Then it joins in with the melody. Which instrument is this?
b) Give the name of another wind instrument which also joins in playing the melody of this *Air*.

JOSEPH HAYDN

A.

a) Where was Haydn born? Was his family musical?

b) In which city did he become a choirboy?

c) For thirty years of his life, Haydn worked for a rich Hungarian family called Esterházy. What was he expected to do there as Kapellmeister (or 'director of music')?

d) Which country did Haydn visit towards the end of his life?

e) What kind of music did he take with him to be performed there?

f) How did Haydn conduct the orchestra when these pieces were played?

g) Can you name another composer who lived at the same time as Haydn?

B.

a) Name these four percussion instruments which take part in Haydn's *Symphony No. 100 in G (the 'Military' Symphony)*:

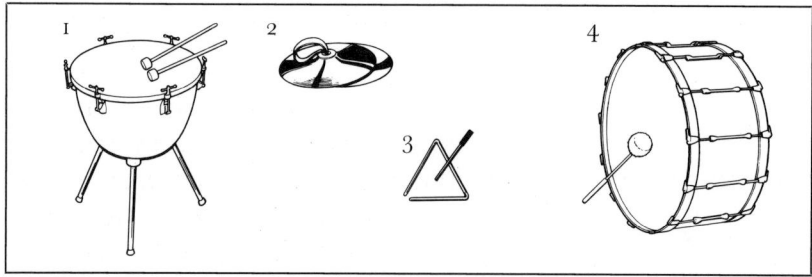

b) Which of these two drums can play *notes* – and which can really only make a *noise*?

c) Can you think of another kind of drum, not drawn in the box? Does it play notes, or only make a noise?

d) Only one of these kinds of drum was a regular member of the orchestra in Haydn's time. Which one is that?

e) Write down two ways of playing each of the percussion instruments drawn in the box.

f) Make drawings of these percussion instruments. Write the name of each instrument underneath your drawing.

C. What kind of pieces of music are these?

| a piano trio | a string quartet | a symphony |

LUDWIG VAN BEETHOVEN

A.

a) Which instruments did Beethoven learn to play as a boy?

b) How did his father make it clear that he wanted his son to become a famous musician?

c) In which city did Beethoven live for most of his life?

d) Which two famous Austrian composers were already living there? How did Beethoven come to meet each of these composers?

e) How do we know that Beethoven was not easily satisfied with the music he composed?

f) Before he was thirty, Beethoven realised that he was becoming deaf. How did this affect his behaviour towards his friends?

g) How did it affect his life as a musician?

h) How many symphonies did Beethoven compose?

B. Name these instruments which Beethoven includes in his *'Pastoral' Symphony*:

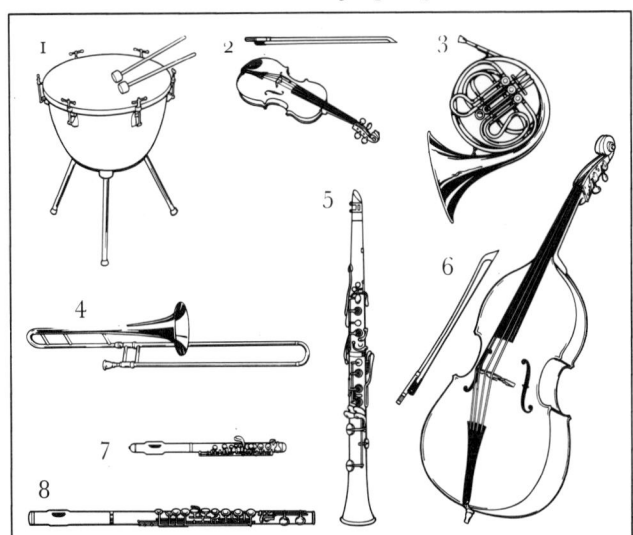

To which section of the orchestra does each instrument belong?

C. Copy this drawing of a violin – but instead of the numbers, write the names of the parts of the violin which are shown by the arrows.

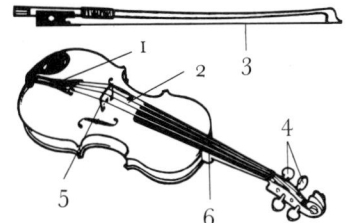

Violin

a) How are the strings fixed on a violin?

b) Describe two ways of playing a violin.

c) Name other instruments which belong to the same section of the orchestra.

D. Look at the Storm music from Beethoven's *'Pastoral' Symphony*, printed on page 20.

a) This is a page taken from the conductor's 'score'. What kind of book is that?

b) The lines of music for the instruments are arranged according to the four sections of the orchestra. In what order do these sections come, from top to bottom of the page?

c) Which instrument is playing a 'roll' to suggest the rumbling of thunder?

d) Which instruments play the same notes, over and over again, in groups of four and five?
Are they playing high notes, or low notes?

e) Name two kinds of instrument which are playing this jerky rhythm:

f) Which two sections of the orchestra are playing long-held notes?

g) At this point in the music, the storm has not yet reached its height. Beethoven is keeping two kinds of instrument in reserve for later. Which instruments are they?

53

FRYDERYK CHOPIN

A.

a) Chopin's pieces are mostly for just one instrument. Which instrument is this?

b) In 1830 Chopin left Poland, never to return. How old was he?

c) In which country did he live for the rest of his life?

d) Name two important friends he made – and say how each of these men had become famous.

e) Chopin became very ill. Where did he go, hoping his health might improve? Why was this not successful?

f) How old was Chopin when he died? Where was he buried?

B. Match the words in the boxes to the instruments in the circles. Some of the words may belong to more than one of these instruments.

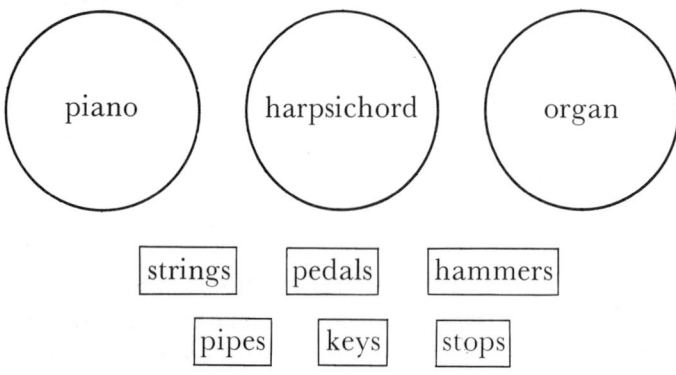

Explain how each of these three instruments makes its sounds.

C. Here are some of the kinds of piece for which Chopin became famous. Match each title with one of the descriptions.

waltz	a) usually quite a difficult piece, meant to improve a player's technique in some way
étude	b) this title means a 'night-piece'
polonaise	c) a lilting dance, with 3 beats to a bar
nocturne	d) a Polish processional dance, with 3 beats to a bar, and very stately dance-steps

GIUSEPPE VERDI

A. Copy this framework. Then, using the clues given on the right, fill in the missing words.

1. Verdi's christian name.
2. Besides music, Verdi had a great love for . . . . . .
3. Verdi's nationality.
4. Name of the hero in *Il Trovatore*.
5. Name of the heroine.
6. Noisy percussion instruments used by Verdi!
7. *Il Trovatore* means 'The . . . . . .'
8. This is the brother of 'Il Trovatore'.
9. Another opera composed by Verdi.
10. Music heard at the beginning of an opera.
11. Gypsy woman in *Il Trovatore*.

B. A new recording is being made of Verdi's opera, *Il Trovatore*. Draw and colour a picture which might be used on the record sleeve.

JOHANN STRAUSS THE YOUNGER

A.
a) In which city did the Strauss family live?
b) As a boy, how did Johann Strauss the Younger show that he was determined to become a musician like his father?
c) Johann Strauss the Younger is most famous for the many waltzes he composed. What kind of dance is a waltz?
d) Can you give the title of another waltz he composed – besides *The Blue Danube*?
e) Strauss composed other kinds of dances, such as polkas. What is a polka?
f) He also composed several operettas. What is an operetta?
g) Which two members of the Strauss family shared in composing *Pizzicato Polka*?
h) Can you name any other composers who were born in Austria?

B. Hidden among the letters in this circle are the names of four instruments from the string section of the orchestra. How many can you find? (Use each letter as often as you like.)

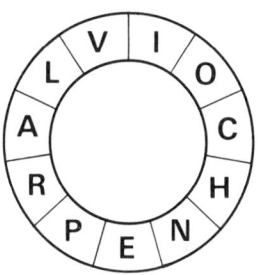

(Which string instrument is *not* included?)

C. Draw and colour a design for a poster to advertise a special concert of music by the Strauss family to be given on New Year's Day.

EDVARD GRIEG

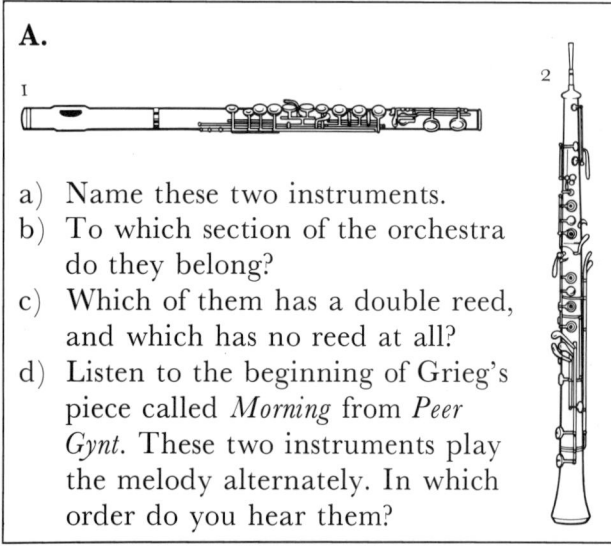

A.

1 2

a) Name these two instruments.
b) To which section of the orchestra do they belong?
c) Which of them has a double reed, and which has no reed at all?
d) Listen to the beginning of Grieg's piece called *Morning* from *Peer Gynt*. These two instruments play the melody alternately. In which order do you hear them?

B.

a) In which section of the orchestra would you find the bassoon?
b) What part of a bassoon do we call the 'crook'? Why do you think we give it this name?
c) Where is the reed fixed on a bassoon?
d) Has the bassoon a single reed, or a double reed?
e) Which other instrument has the same sort of reed?
f) Listen to the beginning of Grieg's piece called *In the Hall of the Mountain King*. What kind of sound does the bassoon make?
g) Make your own drawing of a bassoon. Add these words, with arrows pointing to the correct places on your drawing:

| reed | crook | keys |

Bassoon

C.
Either: draw and colour a scene from *Peer Gynt*.

Or: Imagine you are Peer Gynt exploring the dark caves beneath the mountains. Describe how the trolls surround you – and then slowly begin to close in. . . .

D. Using Grieg's music as a background, act out the scene in the Hall of the Mountain King.

The music ends as Peer is dragged forward before the throne of the evil Mountain King. This is how the scene continues:

Troll Courtiers:	What shall we do to him?
A Young Troll:	Let me wrench off his fingers!
A Troll Maiden:	Let me chew off his lips!
Another:	I'll tear out his hair!
A Troll with two heads:	I'll suck out his eyes!
A Troll Witch with a ladle:	Shall we boil him to a broth?
Another Witch with an axe:	Or spit him and roast him?

What do you think happens next?

E. In this musical framework, for a change, the answers are already filled in. Make up your own clue for each one.

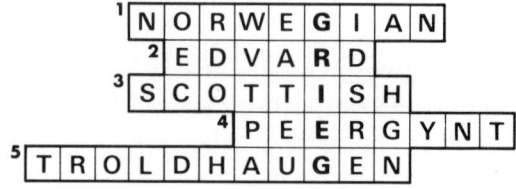

F. Grieg was keenly interested in the folk music of his country. He arranged many Norwegian folk tunes for piano or for orchestra. Here is a Norwegian melody he discovered, arranged here for recorders to play:

Cow Keeper's Tune

(*It is possible to omit the treble recorder part in this piece.)

EDWARD ELGAR

A.

a) Where was Elgar born?

b) How did he learn about music as a boy?

c) Which instruments did he learn to play?

d) What was his first composition which made him really famous?

e) Can you name any other English composers?

B.

1

2

6

slide skin reed
mouthpiece
valves snare keys
tuning pegs
strings bridge bell

3

5

4

a) Name these six instruments, which you would hear in a performance of Elgar's *Pomp and Circumstance March No. 1*.

b) Match each word in the box to the instruments. (You will find that some words belong to more than one instrument.)

C. Here is a plan showing how Elgar builds up the music of his *Pomp and Circumstance March No. 1*:

Tune **A**	Tune **B**	Tune **A**	Tune **B**	Coda

Listen again to this music. How does Elgar make Tune **B** sound different when it comes round for the second time?

D. 'I've a tune that will knock 'em flat!'

Listen again to Elgar's March – if possible, in a recording made at the last night of the Promenade Concerts in London.

Join with the audience in singing the words of 'Land of Hope and Glory' (the words are printed on page 36).

E. Among the letters around the circle, find the name of the instrument drawn in the centre – and also two important parts of this instrument. (Some letters may have to be used more than once.)

F. Design and colour the sleeve for a new record of march music, which will soon be on sale.

ISAAC ALBÉNIZ

A. Using an atlas, see if you can find these places which Albéniz visited when he was a boy:

Spain: Barcelona; Madrid
France: Paris
Argentina (South America): Buenos Aires
Costa Rica (Central America): San José
United States of America: San Francisco and New York
England: Liverpool; London

B. Copy this drawing of a guitar – but instead of the numbers, write the names of the parts of the guitar which are shown by the arrows.

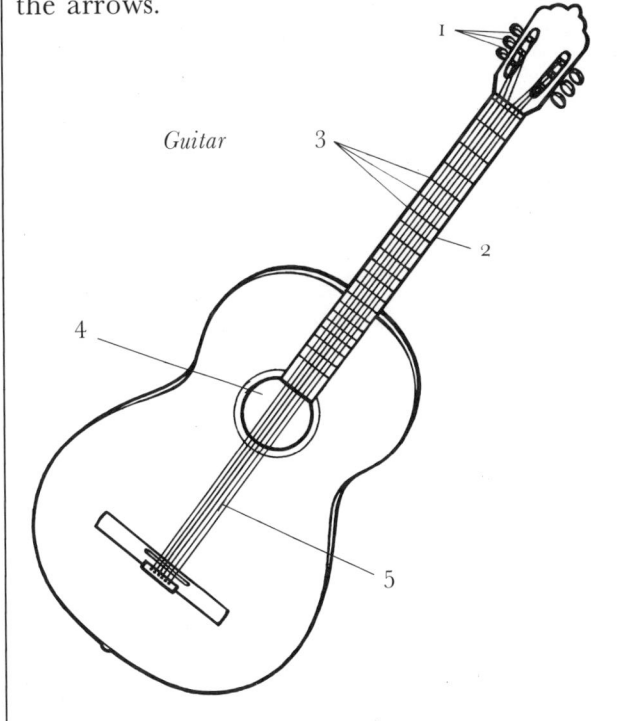

Guitar

C. Imagine that you are Albéniz at the age of fourteen, and that you are being interviewed by a reporter from a Spanish newspaper. Tell the story of your travels and adventures.

D. Copy this framework. Then, using the clues, see if you can fill in the missing words.

```
       1 A
   2     L
     3   B
     4   E
 5       N
     6   I
   7     Z
```

1. Dance from Spain, or Argentina.
2. A region of Southern Spain.
3. Conductor friend of Albéniz who arranged pieces from *Iberia* for full orchestra.
4. These show a guitarist where to press down the strings.
5. *and* 6. Typically Spanish instruments.
7. The famous Hungarian composer and pianist who taught Albéniz for a while.

E. Hidden among the letters around this circle are the names of at least five instruments beginning with the letter 'C'. How many can you find? (Use each letter as often as you like.)

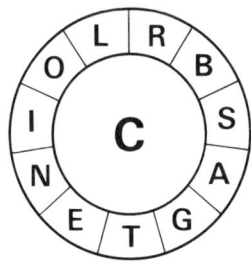

F. Design a cover for a copy of the music of

Either: *Seguidillas* (Castillian Dance) by Isaac Albéniz

Or: *El Corpus en Sevilla* (Easter Festival in Seville) by Isaac Albéniz

SERGEY PROKOFIEV

A.

a) Name these instruments which take part in *Peter and the Wolf* by Prokofiev:

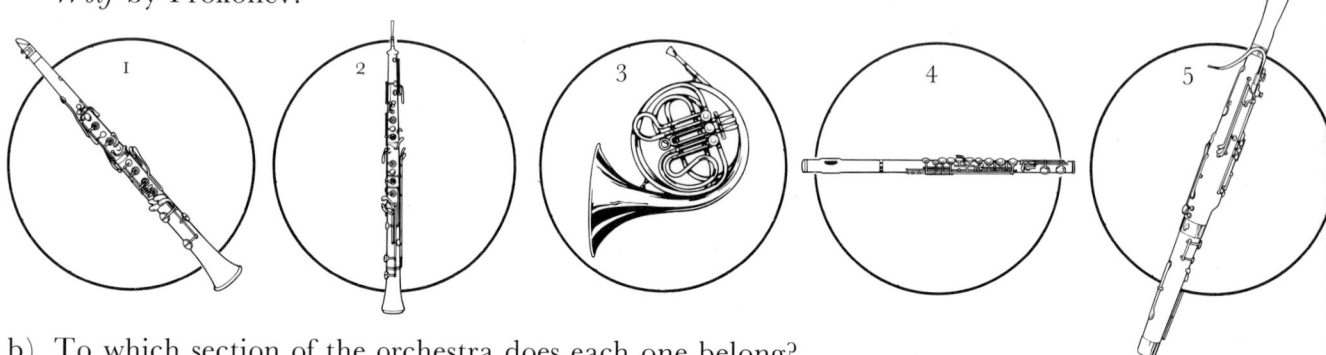

b) To which section of the orchestra does each one belong?

B. Match each of these characters from *Peter and the Wolf* to the instruments drawn in the circles:

| Bird | Cat | Duck | Grandfather | Wolf |

C. Here are five tunes from *Peter and the Wolf*:

a) Match each tune to an instrument drawn on this page.
b) To which character in the story does each tune belong?

D. One character in the story is not mentioned in the boxes on the opposite page. Which character is it? Which instruments do you hear each time this character's tune is played?

E.

Either: tell, in your own words, the story of Peter and the Wolf, drawing and colouring some pictures to illustrate your work;

Or: draw and colour a design for the sleeve of a record of:

> *Peter and the Wolf*
> A Musical Tale for Children
> by Sergey Prokofiev

F. Copy out this framework. Then, using the clues below, fill in the missing words. All the answers are in some way connected with instruments in the woodwind section of the orchestra.

1. This is the smallest instrument in the woodwind section.
2. And this is its 'elder brother'.
3. Gruff, deep-sounding woodwind instrument.
4. A clarinet has one – but a flute does not.
5. The player blows into or across this.
6. A larger, deeper-sounding kind of oboe.
7. A woodwind player uses these in order to make the different notes.
8. A woodwind player needs a lot of this!

G. Here are three more instruments which are heard in *Peter and the Wolf*. Name each one.

    1   2   3

What part do the second and third instruments play in the story of Peter and the Wolf?

H. Hidden in the square are the names of at least twenty instruments – including all those you hear in a performance of *Peter and the Wolf*, and several others as well. They may be horizontal, vertical or diagonal. Some may be spelt backwards, or even upside down. How many can you find?

```
K E T T L E D R U M S
T M S E V I O L I N S
R U N P I C C O L O A
O R A M R O L L E C B
M D R U Z A F L U T E
B S E R B L H B E L L
O S T T N O O S S A B
N A U G R I B G K B U
E B B N Z V O W Z M O
C L A R I N E T Q Y D
S I A L G N A R O C X
```

Afterwards, make four columns with these headings:

  Strings   Woodwind   Brass   Percussion

Then take each instrument you have found, and write its name in the correct column.

AARON COPLAND

A. Make a copy of this framework. Then, using the clues below, see if you can fill in the missing words.

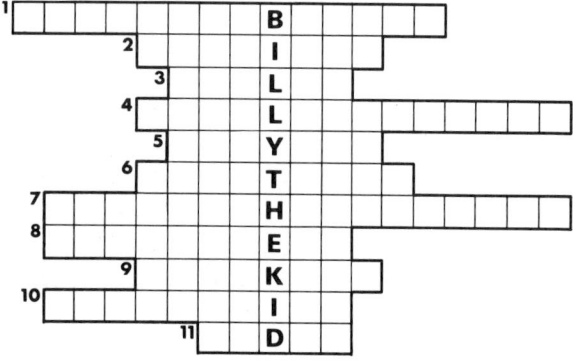

1. Billy the Kid's real name.
2. Copland's nationality.
3. Music in which a story is told by dancing and gestures.
4. This was one of Billy's crimes (2 words).
5. Billy was born here.
6. The number of notches on Billy's pistol.
7. Another ballet by Aaron Copland (2 words).
8. Billy's one-time friend – later his killer!
9. Where Copland was born.
10. Billy lived here for a while (2 words).
11. Copland's other cowboy ballet.

B. Draw and colour a set of pictures, telling about the life and death of Billy the Kid.

Write a sentence or two underneath each picture. Afterwards, listen again to Copland's music. Have you included all the important events in the story of Billy the Kid?

C. Hidden among the letters around the circle are the names of three instruments belonging to the brass section of the orchestra. Can you find all three? (Use each letter as often as you like.)

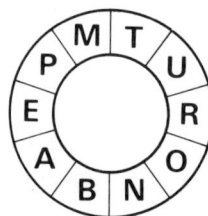

Which instrument from the brass section is *not* included among the letters around the circle?

Quizzes and Puzzles

1. Match each piece to its composer. Then add each composer's first name, and his country.

Peter and the Wolf
The Blue Danube Waltz
Billy the Kid
Music for 'Peer Gynt'
The 'Pastoral' Symphony

Grieg
Copland
Beethoven
Prokofiev
Strauss

2. Hidden among the letters in this square are five composers – and also each composer's country. They may be horizontal, vertical or diagonal. Some may even be spelt backwards or upside down! Can you find them all?

```
P U R C E L L V Y
A C S H Z B E A T
C B S O K R W G E
I A U P D R J R N
R N A I O Z Q I G
E D R N A L Y E L
M I T A L Y A G A
A U S T R I A N N
R O C O P L A N D
```

3. Go through the musical maze – always moving forwards. By passing over letters once only, come out of the maze with a composer.

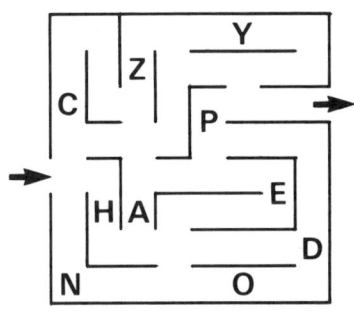

4. As you travel around this spiral, the last letter of each answer becomes the first letter of the next.

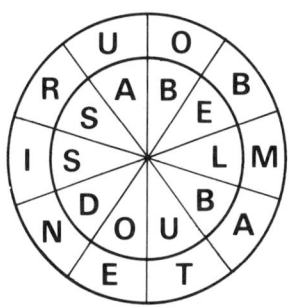

1. This Italian word means 'rather quickly'.
2. An 'opening piece' – perhaps played at the beginning of an opera, or a concert.
3. This composer wrote several marches called *Pomp and Circumstance*.
4. Important to oboes, clarinets and bassoons.
5. Another name for a snare drum.
6. Handel's best known oratorio.
7. An instrument whose strings are plucked.
8. The Italian word which means 'plucked'.
9. A play set to music, acted and sung.
10. Name of a Spanish composer.

5. On this dial, find the names of four instruments – one from each section of the orchestra.

6. Fill in the dashes to find 6 composers:

B–E–H–V–N   G–I–G   –A–D–L
P–R–E–L   –H–P–N   C–P–A–D

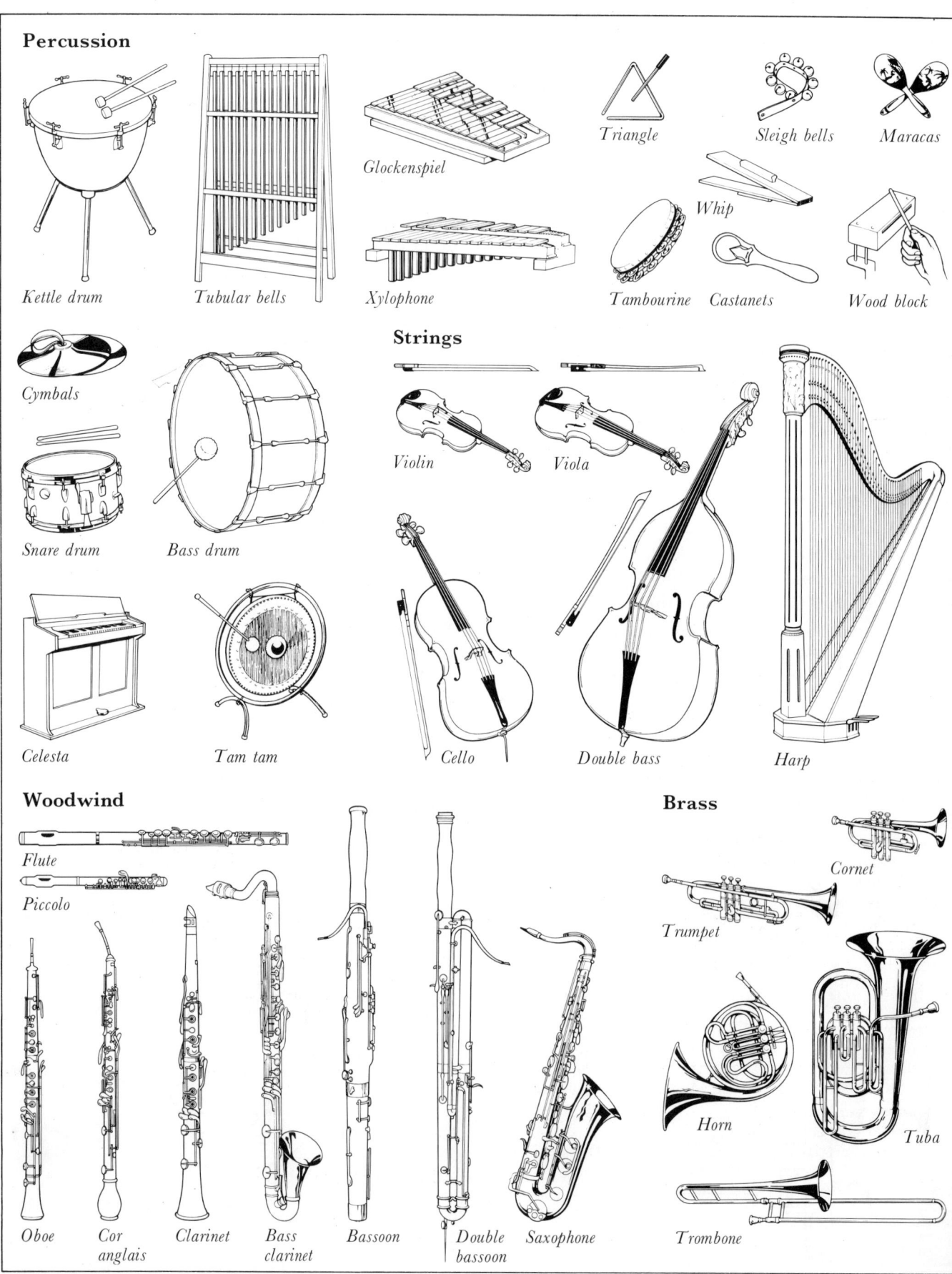

Percussion

Kettle drum *Tubular bells* *Glockenspiel* *Xylophone* *Triangle* *Sleigh bells* *Maracas*

Whip *Tambourine* *Castanets* *Wood block*

Cymbals *Snare drum* *Bass drum*

Celesta *Tam tam*

Strings

Violin *Viola* *Cello* *Double bass* *Harp*

Woodwind

Flute *Piccolo*

Oboe *Cor anglais* *Clarinet* *Bass clarinet* *Bassoon* *Double bassoon* *Saxophone*

Brass

Cornet *Trumpet* *Horn* *Tuba* *Trombone*